The Didache

The Didache

Text, Translation, Analysis, and Commentary

Aaron Milavec

A Michael Glazier Book

LITURGICAL PRESS

Collegeville, Minnesota

www.litpress.org

A Michael Glazier Book published by the Liturgical Press.

Cover design by Ann Blattner.

2	3	4	5	6	7	8

Library of Congress Cataloging-in-Publication Data

Didache. English and Greek.
  The Didache : text, translation, analysis, and commentary / Aaron Milavec.
    p. cm.
  "A Michael Glazier book."
  Includes bibliographical references.
  ISBN 0-8146-5831-8 (alk. paper)
  1. Christian ethics—Early works to 1800. 2. Church—Early works to 1800.
  3. Didache. 4. Christian ethics—History—Early church, ca. 30–600.
  5. Church—History of doctrines—Early church, ca. 30–600.
  I. Milavec, Aaron, 1938– II. Title.

BS2940.T4A3 2004
270.1—dc21

2003051664

To my beloved Deborah

Her presence is the Breath of God

lifting up and caressing me

as my feeble words take flight.

Contents

Introduction

The *Didache* represents the preserved oral tradition whereby mid-first-century house churches detailed the step-by-step transformation by which gentile converts were to be prepared for full active participation in their assemblies. As an oral tradition, the *Didache* encapsulated the lived practice by which non-Jews were initiated into the altered habits of perceiving, judging, and acting characteristic of one branch of the Jesus movement during the mid-first century.

This *Didache* reveals more about how Christians saw themselves and how they lived their everyday lives than any book in the Christian Scriptures. It is not a gospel and, accordingly, it does not attempt to offer guidance by narrating a life of Jesus. In fact, it is older than the canonical gospels and was written in the generation following the death of Jesus when the message of Jesus was not yet encapsulated in stories about Jesus. Nor is the *Didache* a letter like the writings of Paul. In fact, the *Didache* was created at the time of Paul's mission to the gentiles, but it shows not the slightest awareness of that mission or of the theology that undergirded it.

The *Didache* is an anonymous document. Like so many other early Christian books, it did not belong to or originate with a single individual. It belonged to various communities of householders who had received a Way of Life revealed to them by the Father through his servant Jesus. Given the manifest clues of orality within the *Didache* itself, one can be quite certain that it was originally composed orally and that it circulated on the lips of the members of this community for a good many years before any occasion arose that called for a scribe to prepare a textual version.

The *Didache* did not originally have any title. When it was used, everyone knew what it was and how it was to be applied. When the written copy did finally get a title it was called "The Training of the

Lord Through the Twelve Apostles to the Gentiles." Scholars today have abbreviated this long title as **Didache** (usually pronounced "Did-ah-Kay")—the Greek word for the systematic training that a mentor (or a master craftsworker) would give to an understudy (apprentice). This was a remarkably fitting working title even though, as the commentary will show, it has not been adequately appreciated or understood.

The **Didache** represents the first concerted attempt by householders (Crossan 1998) to adapt the way of Jesus to the exigencies of family, occupation, home—the very things that Jesus and his wandering apostles had left behind (Theissen 1977). Paul did this for the communities he founded. The twelve apostles undoubtedly did this for the community at Jerusalem. From Paul, however, we have only occasional letters. From the Twelve we have nothing. The Acts of the Apostles gives only passing details regarding community life in the Jerusalem church and in the churches founded by Paul. The **Didache**, in contrast, offers a full-blown description of nearly every aspect of community life:

> One overhears a candidate being trained from scratch by a mentor who becomes his beloved "father" or "mother." One witnesses the fasting and the solemn rite of baptism, preferably by immersion in flowing water. One overhears the daily prayers and the weekly eucharist—both of which are outlined in full detail. One learns how visiting prophets were a blessing and a danger at the same time. One comes to understand how manual work, the sharing of resources, and the cultivation of gratitude worked together to provide a mainstay for individual wellbeing within a community. One learns how the confession of failings, the correction of backsliders, and the shunning of recalcitrant members worked to maintain the community's standards of excellence and to insure that their sacrifice was pure. Finally, one discovers how a community poised on the threshold of the Kingdom of God shared the same passionate expectation of God's future Jesus had preached to the Jewish peasants and fishermen of Galilee (Milavec, *Didache* 2003, ix).

Initially the ordering of the material in the **Didache** may seem ragged and confusing. Upon careful examination, however, one can discover the organizational thread that accounts for the flow of topics and reveals the marvelous unity hidden below the surface from beginning to end. This is the same organizational thread that those who originally recited the **Didache** relied upon for ordering their recitation. The organizational thread is this: the **Didache** unfolds the comprehensive, step by step program used for the formation of a gentile convert. By following the order of the *Didache*, mentors training novices were assured of following the progressive, ordered, and psychologically sound path that master trainers had effectively culled from their own successful practice in apprenticing novices. From the vantage point of the novice the ordering of events within the *Didache* reveals how a candidate came to progressively enlarge those habits of judgment and ritualized experiences required for a full and active participation in the community. Needless to say, this organizational thread will not be entirely evident at first reading. With time, however, one will come away with the growing satisfaction of noticing how, at every point, nothing comes too early, nothing comes too late, everything comes in just its proper place.

Christians have come to regard the books of the Christian Scriptures (New Testament) as including all the authentic writings produced by the Jesus movement during the first century. Sad to say, this judgment is not correct. The *Gospel of Thomas* and the Q-Gospel represent two instances of first-century productions not found in the canon. Nor, for that matter, do the Christian Scriptures say anything of the thriving community at Qumran or of the books in the fabulous two-thousand-year-old library nearby that was discovered in 1943 and has come to be known as the Dead Sea Scrolls. But think again of the Pauline letters. While Luke claims, in typical Hellenistic fashion, to have gathered primary sources (Luke 1:1-4), these sources apparently did not include even a single copy of any of Paul's letters, which, at the time of his writing, had been in circulation for over twenty years. The modern reader, consequently, need not be entirely dismayed that the Acts of the Apostles makes no reference to the *Didache* and that, even after being circulated and used regionally, the *Didache* failed to have enough clout to gain inclusion in the fourth-century universal canons of books (the New Testament).

The Modern Rediscovery of the *Didache*

Books deteriorate and are destroyed with the ravages of time. Even books hand-printed on prepared sheepskin seldom last for twenty generations. Thus it is not so surprising that the revival of classical learning known as the Renaisssance was unable to bring forward even a single known copy of the *Didache*. Then, to the surprise of everyone, a single complete copy of the *Didache* was found in 1873. As it happened,

Archbishop Philotheos Bryennios was browsing in the library of the Greek Convent of the Holy Sepulchre in Istanbul when, by chance, he noticed the text of the **Didache** hidden away within a bound collection of early church writings. This discovery was all the more unexpected since various professional catalogers had already systematically combed through the codices on these shelves and had failed to notice the presence of the **Didache**.

Bryennios was forty at the time and had spent his early years teaching church history before being advanced to various administrative and pastoral posts in the Greek Orthodox Church. In fact, Bryennios had been appointed as bishop a year earlier and was actively committed to church reform. Thus, even with his increased responsibilities, he deliberately made time for his scholarship because he wished to actively foster "a piety built upon a clear understanding of the transformations that modern society requires of the ancient churches" (cited in Sabatier, *La Didache* 1). Given the wide range of interests and occupations calling for Bryennios' attention, another ten years passed before he fully recognized and finally published his extraordinary find.

Almost overnight, scholars in Europe, England, and America expressed their complete astonishment that such an ancient and important work had finally surfaced. When the first English translation prepared by Hitchcock and Brown was released on 20 March 1884 in New York bookstores, five thousand copies were sold on the first day (Sabatier, *La Didache* 5). On the other hand, some scholars regarded Bryennios' find as too good to be true and rejected it as "a modern forgery" (see Hitchcock and Brown, *The Teaching* v). It was almost as though a document lost for nearly fifteen hundred years and overlooked repeatedly by scholars cataloging the Istanbul library was not allowed to show up so unexpectedly. After a few years, however, the judgment of authenticity prevailed and skeptics were silenced.

The **Didache** is approximately one-third the length of Mark's Gospel. It now resides in the library of the Orthodox Patriarch of Jerusalem where is has been catalogued as Codex Hierosolymitanus 54. The vocabulary and grammar are typical of popular Greek *(koinē)* used in the first century. "The style is simple, natural, terse, sententious, and popular" (P. Schaff, *Oldest Church Manual* 96). As to its vocabulary:

> The **Didache** contains 2190 words. Its vocabulary comprises 552 words . . . 504 are New Testament words, 497 are classical, and 479 occur in the Septuagint. 15 [words] occur for the first time in

the *Didache*, but are found in later writers. 1 [word, *prosexomologein*, found in 14:1] occurs only in the *Didache* [but its meaning can be easily surmised by combining known words] (ibid. 97).

The Unity of the *Didache* and Its Independence from Known Gospels

In the course of the last fifteen years my ideas regarding the *Didache* have changed many times. During this period, however, two convictions have stood the test of time and have shaped my approach to interpreting the *Didache*:

1. *Unity of the Didache.* Up to this point a unified reading of the *Didache* has been impossible because the prevailing assumption has been that the *Didache* was created in stages, with the compiler splicing together pre-existing documents with only a minimum of editing. The end result, therefore, was a complex (or even a haphazard) collage that joined together bits and pieces of traditional material coming from unidentified communities and/or unknown authors. The conviction undergirding my commentary, however, is that the *Didache* has a marvelous unity from beginning to end that, up to this point, has gone unnoticed. Once it is revealed, however, the reader quickly discovers how seemingly incidental clues and abrupt jumps follow a marvelously constructed ordering of the whole. Accordingly, this present study of the *Didache* will expend only passing energy on issues of source and redaction criticism and will concentrate on hearing the text as a whole and endeavoring to discern the organizational thread that guided the framers in the ordering of their material.

2. *Independence of the Didache from the Gospels.* The *Didache* has been widely understood as citing either Matthew's Gospel or some combination of the Matthean or Lucan traditions. From this vantage point it followed that the date of composition had to be set beyond the 80s and the synoptic material could be used to help interpret and understand the *Didache*. Thanks to my work with Willy Rordorf, I came to an early appreciation of the possibility that the *Didache* might have been created without any dependence upon a known gospel. My extensive study of this issue (Milavec, *Didache* [2003], Chapter 11) demonstrates that the internal logic, theological orientation, and pastoral practice of the *Didache* run decisively counter to what one finds within the received gospels.

The repercussions of this conclusion are of decisive importance for the dating and interpretation of the *Didache*. If one supposes an early-second-century origin for the *Didache*, for example, one is naturally disposed to find points where the *Didache* shows dependence upon one or more known gospels then in circulation. The widespread supposition of gospel dependence, therefore, has blocked most scholars from seriously entertaining the possibility of a mid-first-century origin of the *Didache*. The supposition of gospel dependence has also encouraged an "inappropriate" interpretation of the text. If one presumes, for example, that the *Didache* made use of Matthew's Gospel one could justifiably make use of Matthew's theology and church practice as sources for clarifying the intent and background of the *Didache*. On the other hand, if one supposes that the *Didache* is independent of Matthew, then it would be unwarranted to use that gospel to clarify obscure segments of a text created outside of its influence. My conclusion that the *Didache* was composed independently of any known gospel thus means that the gospels can provide studies in contrast and comparison, but they cannot be used to fill in the intent of the framers of the *Didache*. Within my commentary, consequently, great importance is placed upon allowing the internal evidence of the text to speak for itself free of the influence of what was believed and what was done elsewhere. The case of the *Didache* is thus comparable to that of the letter to the Hebrews. As soon as it was discovered that Paul was not the author it was likewise required that Hebrews be interpreted based upon its own internal logic and rhetoric, quite independent of the theology of the authentic Pauline letters.

Norms for Establishing a Working Greek Text

The Greek manuscript discovered by Bryennios is well preserved, carefully written, and employs a score of tachygraphic signs or abbreviations in common use during the Middle Ages when it was copied. The scribe who made the copy identified himself as "Leon, scribe and sinner" and dates the completion of his work as 1056.

J. Rendel Harris (*The Teaching of the Apostles* 1–10) produced a careful transcription of the manuscript in which he expanded the medieval tachygraphic signs. The Greek text found in this book follows the transcription made by Harris as corrected by my own careful examination of a reproduction of the original. In approximately two dozen places

Harris made minor transcription errors (details in Milavec, *Didache*, "How the Greek Manuscript Was Discovered, Transcribed, and Translated"). Furthermore, the Greek manuscript itself contains minor errors: in three places colons were omitted (10:2, 4; 14:3) and in three places short words were omitted (9:4, 10:4, 11:5). These corrections have been widely accepted by current scholars. For the sake of fidelity to the original, however, these minor additions are presented in pointed brackets (< >) to indicate that they were added to the Greek text.

Going beyond this, a long line of scholars has tried to improve the intelligibility of the text by replacing words or phrases with near equivalents. Harris himself gave much attention to a number of substitutions brought forward by Harnack and Hilgenfeld. In the end, however, he preferred not to alter the original text on the following grounds:

> Indeed it must be admitted that with slight exceptions the attempts to emend the text have not been very successful. The most difficult passages have yielded to interpretative skill . . . and this should assure us that any alterations in the text must not be more than moderate if they are to be in any degree acceptable (Harris, *The Teaching of the Apostles* 14).

This, then, is the rule guiding this commentary: *lectio difficilior potior* ("The more difficult reading is preferable"). In my judgment the purpose of the scholar is best served by allowing the singularity of the text to stand out and refraining from harmonizing the text on the basis of what was written or done elsewhere.

Scholars such as Aelred Cody, Willy Rordorf, and Georg Schöllgen have followed this approach to the text very successfully. Jean-Paul Audet, Kurt Niederwimmer, and Klaus Wengst, on the other hand, allow corrections on the basis of comparison with the Latin or Coptic fragments or the *Apostolic Constitutions.* Wengst, in his Greek reconstruction, introduces fifty alterations to the received text (see Bordewijn Dehandschutter, "The Text of the Didache"). In the end this creates a hypothetical hybrid that can never be known ever to have existed or been used.

Even seemingly moderate alterations are suspect. Niederwimmer, for instance, suggests that the unusual word *klasma* ("fragment") in *Did.* 9:3-4 ought to be replaced by the usual word *artos* ("loaf"). Erik Peterson ("Über einige Probleme," 168–69), Arthur Vööbus (*Liturgical Traditions* 89, 146–48), and Klaus Wengst (*Didache* 97–98) agree with him. He explains himself as follows:

> Verse 3 gives the second benediction, the blessing of the bread, introduced by the rubric *peri de tou klasmatos* ["And concerning the fragment"]. This suggests that we should understand *klasma* ["fragment"] to mean the bread broken at the meal celebration. In that case, the plural *peri de tōn klasmatōn* ["And concerning the fragments"] would seem more appropriate. . . . The parallels from later liturgies have *artos* in the analogous location. Peterson has pointed out that *klasma* is a technical term in the eucharistic language of Egypt; it refers to the particle of the host. The expression could then have entered the text at a secondary stage (Niederwimmer, *Didache* 148).

If the technical term *klasma* goes back to the Egyptian liturgy and accordingly hints at a late origin of the **Didache** (Charles Bigg, "Notes on the Didache" [1905] 414), one might be willing to drop the tainted "late word" in favor of the supposed earlier term, namely, *artos*. This substitution in *Did.* 9:3, however, would require that *Did.* 9:5 be altered such that "fragments of bread," or better, "grains of bread" would be scattered over the hills. It makes no sense to scatter a loaf *(artos)*. The substitution allowed by Niederwimmer (as well as by Wengst, Peterson, and Vööbus) thus resolves one difficulty by creating another one.

Going deeper, however, what if it could be shown that the term "fragment" goes back to an ancient Jewish usage whereby the loaf was broken prior to being blessed and thus only a "fragment" was held up as representing the whole? In that case *klasma* would offer a hint of the Hebraic idioms that might once have flourished in the archaic form of the eucharistic liturgy found in the **Didache**. Hence by retaining the more difficult reading of the original one retains the necessity of finding a suitable reason for why this *(klasma)* and not that *(artos)*. Those who would substitute *artos* gain a "quick fix" in terms of intelligibility but lose the precious hint that the **Didache** may contain archaic idioms that were part of its foundation and that, with a little prying, might reveal untold mysteries of its true origins and pastoral genius. I have elected in every case, therefore, to stay with the original.

Norms for Preparing an Analytic, Gender-Inclusive Translation

The Greek transcription and English translation on the following pages have been set out so as to facilitate the reading and analysis of the received text. The Greek manuscript prepared by Leon was presented on continuous lines with little or no space left to indicate the end of words, of sentences, and of sections. To make the Greek text and its English translation more accessible, the following pages group and organize the material in such a way that on first reading the internal logic begins to make itself evident. Thus one can identify units of thought, repetitious patterns, and key transitions that ordinarily only a close study of the text would reveal. This, a technique I learned from Jacob Neusner, is what is meant here by an analytic translation.

The English translation produced here retains the literal Greek meaning without slavishly following the Greek word order and usage. Idioms in the Greek are rendered into English with only small adaptations in order to achieve a close dynamic equivalence without yielding stilted English. Words or phrases placed in brackets serve to clarify the elliptical intent of the Greek while acknowledging that they are absent from the literal Greek text. English words linked together by underlined spaces signal instances where a single Greek word needs to be rendered by a phrase in English. In sum, the English translation in this volume is conservatively constructed so that, in principle, it could be retranslated back into the original Greek.

Since the English language has lost its ability to differentiate between the singular and plural "you," this translation uses "ÿou/ÿour" to signal the plural. Likewise, when the context fails to make it evident that a verb has a plural subject, an umlaut is used to signal the plural form. Thus, for example, "Präy for ÿour enemies" (*Did.* 1:3) allows the English reader to know that the Greek has a plural imperative ("Präy") matched by a plural pronoun ("ÿour").

The post-positive particle *de* is frequently used in Greek to signal a continuation of the foregoing topic. An English-speaking storyteller who links sentences with "and" or "and then" is effectively doing the same thing as a Greek speaker would do. Accordingly, when *de* appears in the Greek, the English translation will render this *de* as "(and)." Placing the "and" in parentheses at the beginning of the sentence indicates that current English style normally avoids it. Where *kai* ("and") is found in the Greek it is consistently rendered as "and" without parentheses. The post-positive particle *de* can sometimes have an adversative sense. In these cases it is rendered into English as "(but)" or "on the other hand." Where *alla* ("but") is found, it is consistently rendered as "but" without any parentheses.

Finally, the Greek language assigns gender to nouns and pronouns somewhat differently than does English. Nouns in English designating "things" are neuter, while nouns designating "living beings" are either masculine or feminine. Greek nouns designating things may be masculine, feminine, or neuter (as in most European languages). When Greek verbs allow for either a male or female subject or a female or male object this will be appropriately signaled by using an inclusive English translation. Overall, the entire **Didache** is 99% inclusive, yet every modern English translation I have yet examined leaves the mistaken impression that "men" were addressing "men" about "manly things" throughout. This translation will demonstrate that "women" were also addressing "women" about "womanly things." This commentary will thus rectify a gender distortion that has misrepresented the intent and use of the **Didache**.

Acknowledgments

The writing of this book would have been impossible without the generous help of many persons. First and foremost I want to honor Jacob Neusner, Michael Polanyi, and Willy Rordorf. Each contributed his special know-how in my quest to understand the *Didache*. Each of their contributions was profound and enduring. Without these giants I would not have had the strong shoulders to stand on, so as to see far.

Carol Andreini, Associate Professor of Classics at North Dakota State University, provided me with a fresh translation of the Greek text at the very beginning of this project in 1988. During the following year, thanks to a Lilly Endowment Grant, we were able to work side by side over a period of weeks, sorting out the nuances of the *koinē* Greek of the *Didache* and identifying classical parallels. While the final form of the translation is my responsibility, its content and consistency reflect her expertise and linguistic insights.

Dozens of colleagues offered me feedback and insights on the many academic papers and public presentations I gave on various topics related to the *Didache*. Among these, John Dominic Crossan, codirector of the Jesus Seminar, Philip Culbertson of St. John's College (New Zealand), and Jonathan Draper of the University of Natal (South Africa) deserve special recognition due to our hours of exchange and our shared concern to unearth the social questions behind the *Didache*. Dennis C. Duling, Deirdre Good, Rabbi Simchah Roth, Richard Sarason, and Eileen Schuller offered me invaluable feedback on key questions along the way. The students in my *Didache* seminars, both in Cincinnati and in Neuchâtel, are also to be recognized for their sustained attention to the internal structure of the text and their creative efforts to draw out its pastoral genius. I frequently came away from class realizing that I had learned more than I had taught.

During the long course of my research I was grateful to have received financial assistance and public recognition in the form of grants and faculty fellowships from the Association of Theological Schools, the National Endowment for the Humanities, and the Lilly Foundation (twice). My thanks also go to Linda and Gilbert Bartholomew for their sustained personal and financial assistance. Recognition is also due to the library staff of United Theological Seminary (Dayton) for offering me unlimited access to their academic collection, and to the Rev. James Christy, pastor of the Greene Street Methodist Church (Piqua), for providing me urgently needed office space.

As this book was being fashioned, a companion website, www.Didache.info, was taking shape by its side. The latter promises to enable students, pastors, and scholars to find a relaxed, user-friendly forum for exchanging insights and evaluating fresh discoveries occasioned by study of the former. I am indebted to Martin Heine (www.lightartvision.de) for designing an attractive, state-of-the-art home page that I have been able to modify and expand for this purpose. L. C. Macouno (www.alienhelpdesk.com) has greatly assisted me in setting up a flawless discussion forum. Finally, my appreciation goes to the Center for Innovative Learning at the University of Victoria (British Columbia) for showing me that book-learning and interactive-web-learning are intimate companions. They are the attractive twin sisters nurturing the love of learning in our electronic age.

Linda Maloney of Liturgical Press has been singularly helpful in correcting the manuscript and guiding it through the publishing process. Even in our initial exchanges Linda saw the need for making available to a wide audience the analytical, gender-inclusive translation of the *Didache* that formed the foundation of my thousand-page commentary with Paulist Press. Kathy Zdroik laboriously typed and proofread the Greek text. Finally, Linda had me draft "Questions for Review and Study" and offer study aids that would make this small volume a user-friendly resource bringing together literary criticism and sociological analysis in order to reconstruct the faith, hope, and life of those mid-first-century Christian communities using the *Didache*.

My beloved wife, Deborah Rose-Milavec, sustained me throughout the writing of this book. More than anyone else, she encouraged me to write not just for scholars, pastors, and students, but for ordinary people as well. Deb is the former director of a women's shelter in Sidney. Even the victims of domestic violence, Deb continually reminded me, might well have a spiritual hunger for the *Didache*. Ordinary people need to be engaged by religious institutions without being tyrannized, nourished without being force-fed, listened to without being patronized. This is the undercurrent quietly running below the surface of the *Didache*. The whole subtext speaks of ordinary holiness accomplished by ordinary people in extraordinarily difficult times. The battered women passing through Deb's shelter may well be the first to understand this and to welcome such a healing message into their lives.

I want to acknowledge the courage and pastoral sensitivity of those capable pastors of the mid-first-century who collaboratively crafted the *Didache* as their matrix for training gentiles longing to acquire the skills to walk in the Way of Life revealed by our Father/Mother. In the stillness of the night these pastors spoke to me. I was frequently so dazzled with their practical and divinely-inspired genius that I was forced to rise from my warm bed, grab a bathrobe, and quickly capture their fading voices on the chilly keys of my word processor. May they be blessed in their sleep, and blessed in their awakening!

Last but not least I acknowledge "the four winds" (*Did.* 10:5) that refreshed my soul while writing this book by ushering in quiet layers of fog, fierce thunderstorms, and dancing snowflakes. For those trees whose lives were extinguished in order that this book might have pages, I offer my humble prayer. Likewise, I would be remiss if I did not ask pardon for the excessive suffering inflicted on birds, animals, and fish as a byproduct of the modern technology of forestry and paper production. Nearly all pulp mills in Europe recycle the staggering amounts of water necessary for paper production. In the United States and Canada, however, even while mills have taken some measures to reduce their toxic emissions, every mill hourly discharges thousands of gallons of contaminated water into the natural environment. Wildlife downstream without access to bottled water and children of poorer families without access to a swimming pool are *at risk*. In the state of Washington a full third of the total industrial toxic discharge comes from local paper mills. Bald eagles, the proud icons of American freedom, helplessly watch their young die, even though they are nesting miles from those contaminated waters. The tragedy is that here in "the land of the free, the home of the brave," the very words heralding the Way of Life are printed on the inexpensive paper made possible by an industry practicing the Way of Death.

THE DIDACHE

διδαχὴ τῶν δώδεκα ἀποστόλων

Διδαχὴ κυρίου διὰ τῶν δώδεκα ἀποστόλων τοῖς ἔθνεσιν·

1:1   ὁδοὶ δύο εἰσί· μία τῆς ζωῆς· καὶ μία τοῦ θανάτου·
      διαφορὰ δὲ πολλὴ μεταξὺ τῶν ὁδῶν·

1:2   ἡ μὲν οὖν ὁδὸς τῆς ζωῆς ἐστιν αὕτη·
         πρῶτον· ἀγαπήσεις τὸν θεὸν τὸν ποιήσαντά σε·
         δεύτερον· τὸν πλησίον σου ὡς σεαυτόν·

         πάντα δὲ ὅσα ἐὰν θελήσῃς μὴ γίνεσθαί σοι·
         καὶ σὺ ἄλλῳ μὴ ποίει·

1:3   τούτων δὲ τῶν λόγων ἡ διδαχή ἐστιν αὕτη·

      εὐλογεῖτε τοὺς καταρωμένους ὑμῖν·
      καὶ προσεύχεσθε ὑπὲρ τῶν ἐχθρῶν ὑμῶν·
      νηστεύετε δὲ ὑπὲρ τῶν διωκόντων ὑμᾶς·
         ποία γὰρ χάρις ἐὰν ἀγαπᾶτε τοὺς ἀγαπῶντας ὑμᾶς;
         οὐχὶ καὶ τὰ ἔθνητο αὐτο ποιοῦσιν <;>
      ὑμεῖς δὲ ἀγαπᾶτο τοὺς μισοῦντας ὑμᾶς·
         καὶ οὐχ ἕξετε ἐχθρόν·

1:4   ἀπέχου τῶν σαρκικῶν καὶ σωματικῶν ἐπιθυμιῶν.

      ἐάν τις σοι δῷ ῥάπισμα εἰς τὴν δεξιὰν σιαγόνα
         στρέψον αὐτῷ καὶ τὴν ἄλλην καὶ ἔσῃ τέλειος·
      ἐὰν ἀγγαρεύσῃ σέ τις μίλιον ἕν
         ὕπαγε μετ᾽ αὐτοῦ δύο·
      ἐὰν ἄρῃ τις τὸ ἱμάτιόν σου
         δὸς αὐτῷ καὶ τὸν χιτῶνα·
      ἐὰν λάβῃ τις ἀπὸ σοῦ τὸ σὸν
         μὴ ἀπαίτει·
            οὐδὲ γὰρ δύνασαι·

Training of the Twelve Apostles

Training of [the] Lord Through the Twelve Apostles for the Gentiles

no grey area

1:1   There are two ways: one of life and one of death!   *Matt 7:13,14*
      (And) [there is] a great difference between the two ways.
      gospels" hard to find "

1:2   [A] On_the_one_hand, then, the way of life is this:
          [1] first: you will love the God who made you;
          [2] second: [you will love] your neighbor as yourself.
      [B] On_the_other_hand [the way of life is this]:
          as many [things] as you might wish not to happen to you,   *Luke 6.31*
          likewise, do not do to another.   *Reverse Golden Rule*

1:3   (And) [for an assimilation] of these words, the training is this:

      [A] spëak_well of the ones speaking_badly of ÿou,
      [B] and präy for ÿour enemies,
      [C] (and) fäst for the ones persecuting ÿou;
          For what merit [is there] if ÿou löve the ones loving ÿou?
          Do not even the gentiles do the same thing?
      [D] ÿou, on_the_other_hand, löve the ones hating ÿou,
          and ÿou will not have an enemy.

1:4   Abstain from fleshly and bodily desires. [How so?]

      [A] if anyone should strike you on the right cheek,
          turn to him/her also the other, and you will be perfect;
      [B] if anyone should press_you_into_service for one mile,   *anger, resentment*
          go with him/her two;
      [C] if anyone should take away your cloak,
          give to him/her also your tunic;
      [D] if anyone should take from you [what is] yours,
          do not ask_for_it_back;
              for you are not even able [to do so].

not doctrine but a way of life an apprenticeship in life

1:5   παντὶ τῷ αἰτοῦντί σε δίδου
        καὶ μὴ ἀπαίτει·
            πᾶσι γὰρ θέλει δίδοσθαι ὁ πατὴρ
            ἐκ τῶν ἰδίων χαρισμάτων·

        μακάριος ὁ διδοὺς κατὰ τὴν ἐντολήν·
            ἀθῶος γάρ ἐστιν·
        οὐαὶ τῷ λαμβάνοντι·
            εἰ μὲν γὰρ χρείαν ἔχων λαμβάνει τις
                ἀθῶος ἔσται·
            ὁ δὲ μὴ χρείαν ἔχων·
                δώσει δίκην·
                    ἵνατί ἔλαβε καὶ εἰς τί·
                    ἐν συνοχῇ δὲ γενόμενος ἐξετασθήσεται
                    περὶ ὧν ἔπραξε·
                    καὶ οὐκ ἐξελεύσεται ἐκεῖθεν·
                    μέχρις οὗ ἀποδῷ τὸν ἔσχατον κοδράντην·
1:6   ἀλλὰ καὶ περὶ τούτου δὲ εἴρηται·
            ἱδρωτάτω ἡ ἐλεημοσύνη σου εἰς τὰς χεῖράς σου
            μέχρις ἂν γνῷς τινι δῷς·

2:1   δευτέρα δὲ ἐντολὴ τῆς διδαχῆς·

2:2   οὐ φονεύσεις·
        οὐ μοιχεύσεις·
        οὐ παιδοφθορήσεις·
        οὐ πορνεύσεις·
        οὐ κλέψεις·
        οὐ μαγεύσεις·
        οὐ φαρμακεύσεις·
        οὐ φονεύσεις τέκνον ἐν φθορᾷ·
        οὐδὲ γεννηθέντα ἀποκτενεῖς·
        οὐκ ἐπιθυμήσεις τὰ τοῦ πλησίον·

1:5   To everyone asking you [for anything], give [it]
and do not ask_for_it_back;
>   for, to all, the Father wishes to give
>   [these things] from his_own free_gifts.

[A] Blessed is the one_giving according to the rule;
>   for he/she is blameless.

[B] Woe to the one_taking;
>   [1] for, on_the_one_hand, if anyone having need takes,
>   he/she will be blameless;
>   [2] on_the_other_hand, the one not having need
>>   [a] will stand trial [on the day of judgment]
>>   [as to] why he/she took and for what [use];
>>   [b] (and) being in prison, he/she will be examined_
>>   thoroughly concerning [the things] he/she has done,
>>   [c] and he/she will not come_out from there
>>   until he/she gives_back the last quadrans.

1:6   [C] But also, concerning this [rule], it has been said:
>   "Let your alms sweat in your hands,
>   until you know to whom you might give [it]."

Careful use of money — totally different than today

2:1   (And) the second rule of the training [is this]:

2:2   [A1] You will not murder,
[A2] you will not commit adultery,
[A3] you will not corrupt_boys,   *paido – child boy*
[A4] you will not have_illicit_sex,   *emphasis is on selling for hire not specific act*
[A5] you will not steal,
[A6] you will not practice_magic,
[A7] you will not make_potions,
[A8] you will not murder offspring by_means_of abortion,   *φθορα*
[A9] (and) you will not kill [him/her] having_been_born,
[A10] you will not desire the things of [your] neighbor.

φθορα ∠ — *moral decay destroy*

2:3   οὐκ ἐπιορκήσεις·
οὐ ψευδομαρτυρήσεις·
οὐ κακολογήσεις·
οὐ μνησικακήσεις·

2:4   οὐκ ἔσῃ διγνώμων· οὐδὲ δίγλωσσος·
παγὶς γὰρ θανάτου ἡ διγλωσσία·

2:5   οὐκ ἔσται ὁ λόγος σου ψευδής οὐ κενός·
ἀλλὰ μεμεστωμένος πράξει·

2:6   οὐκ ἔσῃ πλεονέκτης·
οὐδὲ ἅρπαξ·
οὐδὲ ὑποκριτής·
οὐδὲ κακοήθης·
οὐδὲ ὑπερήφανος·

οὐ λήψῃ βουλὴν πονηρὰν κατὰ τοῦ πλησίον σου·

2:7   οὐ μισήσεις πάντα ἄνθρωπον·
ἀλλὰ οὓς μὲν ἐλέγξεις·
περὶ δὲ ὧν προσεύξῃ·
οὓς δὲ ἀγαπήσεις ὑπὲρ τὴν ψυχήν σου·

2:3   [B1] you will not swear_falsely,
         [B2] you will not bear_false_witness,
         [B3] you will not speak_badly [of anyone],
         [B4] you will not hold_grudges.   *single*

2:4   [B5] You will not be double-minded nor double-tongued,
             for being double-tongued is a snare of death.

2:5   [In sum] your word will not be false nor empty,
             but [will be] fulfilled by action.

2:6   [C1] You will not be covetous,
         [C2] (and) not greedy,
         [C3] (and) not a hypocrite,
         [C4] (and) not bad-mannered,
         [C5] (and) not arrogant.

         [In sum] you will not take an evil plan against your neighbor.

2:7   You will not hate any person,
         [1] but some you will reprove,
         [2] and concerning others you will pray,
         [3] and some you will love more than your soul.

3:1   τέκνον μου φεῦγε ἀπὸ παντὸς πονηροῦ·
      καὶ ἀπὸ παντὸς ὁμοίου αὐτοῦ·

3:2   μὴ γίνου ὀργίλος·
            ὁδηγεῖ γὰρ ἡ ὀργὴ πρὸς τὸν φόνον·
      μηδὲ ζηλωτής·
      μηδὲ ἐριστικός·
      μηδὲ θυμικός·
            ἐκ γὰρ τούτων ἁπάντων φόνοι γεννῶνται·

3:3   τέκνον μου· μὴ γίνου ἐπιθυμητής·
            ὁδηγεῖ γὰρ ἡ ἐπιθυμία πρὸς τὴν πορνείαν·
      μηδὲ αἰσχρολόγος·
      μηδὲ ὑψηλόφθαλμος·
            ἐκ γὰρ τούτων ἁπάντων μοιχεῖαι γεννῶνται·

3:4   τέκνον μου μὴ γίμου οἰωνοσκόπος·
            ἐπειδὴ ὁδηγεῖ εἰς τὴν εἰδωλολατρίαν·
      μηδὲ ἐπαοιδός·
      μηδὲ μαθηματικός·
      μηδὲ περικαθαίρων·
      μηδὲ θέλε αὐτὰ βλέπειν·
            ἐκ γὰρ τούτων ἁπάντων εἰδωλολατρία γεννᾶται·

3:5   τέκνον μου μὴ γίνου ψεύστης·
            ἐπειδὴ ὁδηγεῖ τὸ ψεῦσμα εἰς τὴν κλοπήν·
      μηδὲ φιλάργυρος·
      μηδὲ κενόδοξος·
            ἐκ γὰρ τούτων ἁπάντων κλοπαὶ γεννῶνται·

3:6   τέκνον μου μὴ γίνου γόγγυσος·
            ἐπειδὴ ὁδηγεῖ εἰς τὴν βλασφημίαν·
      μηδὲ αὐθάδης·
      μηδὲ πονηρόφρων·
            ἐκ γὰρ τούτων ἁπάντων βλασφημίαι γεννῶνται·

3:1   My child, flee from every evil
       and from everything like it.

3:2   [A] Do not become angry,
              for anger is_the_path_leading to murder;
           nor envious,
           nor contentious,
           nor hot-headed,
              for, from all these, murders are begotten.

3:3   [B] My child, do not become lustful,
              for lust is_the_path_leading to illicit_sex;
           nor one_using_foul_speech,   *eyes of the opposite sex*
           nor one_looking_up [into the face of a woman],
              for, from all these, adulteries are begotten.

3:4   [C] My child, do not become a diviner,
              since [this] is_the_path_leading to idolatry;
           nor an enchanter,
           nor an astrologer,
           nor a purifier,   *magic purification rites*
           nor [even] wish to see these things,
              for, from all these, idolatry is begotten.   *Playing God*

3:5   [D] My child, do not become false,
              since falsehood is_the_path_leading to theft;
           nor a lover_of_money,   *money, power*
           nor a_seeker_of_glory,
              for, from all these, thefts are begotten.

3:6   [E] My child, do not become a grumbler,
              since [this] is_the_path_leading to blasphemy;
           nor self-pleasing,
           nor evil-minded,
              for, from all these, blasphemies are begotten.

3:7   ἴσθι δὲ πραΰς·
      ἐπεὶ οἱ πραεῖς κληρονομήσουσι τὴν γῆν·

3:8   γίνου μακρόθυμος·
         καὶ ἐλεήμων·
         καὶ ἄκακος·
         καὶ ἡσύχιος·
         καὶ ἀγαθὸς·
         καὶ τρέμων τοὺς λόγους διὰπαντός·
            οὓς ἤκουσας·

3:9   οὐχ ὑψώσεις σεαυτόν·
         οὐδὲ δώσεις τῇ ψυχῇ σου θράσος·
         οὐ κολληθήσεται ἡ ψυχή σου μετὰ ὑψηλῶν·
         ἀλλὰ μετὰ δικαίων καὶ ταπεινῶν ἀναστραφήσῃ·

3:10 τὰ συμβαίνοντά σου ἐνεργήματα ὡς ἀγαθὰ προσδέξῃ·
         εἰδὼς ὅτι ἄτερ θεοῦ οὐδὲν γίνεται·

3:7   But be gentle,   *Matt 5.5*
        since the gentle will inherit the earth.

3:8   [A] Become long-suffering
            and merciful
            and harmless
            and calm
            and good
            and trembling through all [time] at the words
                that you have heard.

3:9   [B] You will not exalt yourself,
            (and) you will not give boldness to your soul.
            Your soul will not be joined with [the] lofty,
            but with [the] just and [the] lowly you will dwell.

3:10   [C] You will accept the experiences befalling you as good things,
            knowing that, apart from God, nothing happens.

4:1   τέκνον μου τοῦ λαλοῦντός σοι τὸν λόγον τοῦ θεοῦ·
       μνησθήσῃ νυκτὸς καὶ ἡμέρας·
       τιμήσεις δὲ αὐτὸν ὡς κύριον·
          ὅθεν γὰρ ἡ κυριότης λαλεῖται
          ἐκεῖ κύριός ἐστιν·
4:2   ἐκζητήσεις δὲ καθ᾽ ἡμέραν τὰ πρόσωπα τῶν ἁγίων·
       ἵνα ἐπαναπαῇς τοῖς λόγοις αὐτῶν·

4:3   οὐ ποιήσεις σχίσμα·
       εἰρηνεύσεις δὲ μαχομένους·
       κρινεῖς δικαίως·
       οὐ λήψῃ πρόσωπον
          ἐλέγξαι ἐπὶ παραπτώμασιν·

4:4   οὐ διψυχήσεις πότερον
       ἔσται ἢ οὔ·

4:5   μὴ γίνου
       πρὸς μὲν τὸ λαβεῖν ἐκτείνων τὰς χεῖρας·

       πρὸς δὲ τὸ δοῦναι συσπῶν·

4:6   ἐὰν ἔχῃς διὰ τῶν χειρῶν σου

       δώσεις λύτρωσιν ἁμαρτιῶν σου·
4:7   οὐ διστάσεις δοῦναι·
       οὐδὲ διδοὺς γογγύσεις·
          γνώσῃ γὰρ τίς ἐστιν ὁ τοῦ μισθοῦ
          καλὸς ἀνταποδότης.

4:8   οὐκ ἀποστραφήσῃ τὸν ἐνδεόμενον·
       συγκοινωνήσεις δὲ
          πάντα τῷ ἀδελφῷ σου·
          καὶ οὐκ ἐρεῖς ἴδια εἶναι·
             εἰ γὰρ ἐν τῷ ἀθανάτῳ κοινωνοί ἐστε,
             πόσῳ μᾶλλον ἐν τοῖς θνητοῖς·

4:1   [A] My child, the one speaking to you the word of God,   *later*
          [1] you will remember night and day,
          [2] (and) you will honor him/her as [the] Lord,
              for where [the] dominion [of the Lord] is spoken of,
              there [the] Lord is.
4:2   [3] (And) you will seek every day the presence of the saints)   *addon*
              in order that you may rest upon their words.

4:3   [B] You will not cause dissention:
          [1] (And) you will reconcile those_fighting;
          [2] you will judge justly;
          [3] you will not take [into account] social_status   *James*
              [when it comes time] to reprove against failings.

4:4   [C] You will not be double-minded whether it [God's future?]
              will be or not.

4:5   [A] Do not become [someone],
          [1] on_the_one_hand, stretching out your hands for_the_
              purpose_of taking,
          [2] on_the_other_hand, withdrawing [them] for_the_
              purpose_of giving.

4:6   [B] If you should have [something] through [the work of] your
              hands,
          you will give [something] ransoming of your sins.
4:7   [1] You will not hesitate to give,
          [2] nor giving will you grumble;
              for you will know who will be giving_back
              excellent recompense [when he comes].

4:8   [C] You will not turn_away the one_being_in_need;
          [1] you will partner-together, on_the_other_hand,
              sharing] all [things] with your brother [sister],
          [2] and you will not say [such things] are your own.
              For, if ÿou are partners in the immortal [things],   *Parable*
              by_how_much more [are you partners] in the mortal   *Knowledge*
              [things].

4:9   οὐκ ἀρεῖς τὴν χεῖρά σου
       ἀπὸ τοῦ υἱοῦ σου ἢ ἀπὸ τῆς θυγατρός σου·
       ἀλλὰ ἀπὸ νεότητος διδάξεις τὸν φόβον τοῦ θεοῦ·

4:10   οὐκ ἐπιτάξεις δούλῳ σου ἢ παιδίσκῃ
       τοῖς ἐπὶ τὸν αὐτὸν θεὸν ἐλπίζουσιν
       ἐν πικρίᾳ σου·
           μήποτε οὐ μὴ φοβηθήσονται τὸν ἐπ᾽ ἀμφοτέροις θεόν·

       οὐ γὰρ ἔρχεται κατὰ πρόσωπον καλέσαι·

       ἀλλ᾽ ἐφ᾽ οὓς τὸ πνεῦμα ἡτοίμασεν·

4:11   ὑμεῖς δὲ οἱ δοῦλοι ὑποταγήσεσθε τοῖς κυρίοις ὑμῶν·
       ὡς τύπῳ θεοῦ ἐν αἰσχύνῃ καὶ φόβῳ·

4:12   μισήσεις πᾶσαν ὑπόκρισιν
       καὶ πᾶν ὃ μὴ ἀρεστὸν τῷ κυρίῳ·

4:13   οὐ μὴ ἐγκαταλίπῃς ἐντολὰς κυρίου·
       φυλάξεις δὲ ἃ παρέλαβες·
       μήτε προστιθεὶς· μήτε ἀφαιρῶν·

4:14   ἐν ἐκκλησίᾳ ἐξομολογήσῃ τὰ παραπτώματά σου·
       καὶ οὐ προσελεύσῃ ἐπὶ πρσευχήν σου ἐν συνειδήσει πονηρᾷ·

       αὕτη ἐστὶν ἡ ὁδὸς τῆς ζωῆς·

4:9   [A] You will not take away your hand
             from your son or from your daughter,
             but from youth you will train [them] in the fear of God.

4:10   [B] You will not command your male or female_slave
             (the ones hoping in the same God [as you])
             in your bitterness,
                 lest they should ever not fear the God [who is] over
                     both [of ÿou],
                 for [God] does not come to call [anyone] according_to
                     [his/her] social_status,
                 but [God calls] those whom the Spirit has made-ready.

4:11   [C] And ÿou, the slaves, will be_subject_to ÿour lords
             as to the image of God in shame and fear.

4:12   [A] You will hate every hypocrisy,
             and everything that is not pleasing to the Lord.

4:13   [B] You will not at all leave_behind the rules of [the] Lord,
             (but) you will guard the things that you have received,
             neither adding nor taking [anything] away.
                 assembly
4:14   [C] In church, you will confess your failings,
             and you will not go to your prayer with a bad conscience.

       This is the Way of Life!

5:1   ἡ δὲ τοῦ θανάτου ὁδός ἐστιν αὕτη·

πρῶτον πάντων πονηρά ἐστι καὶ κατάρας μεστή·

φόνοι·   διπλοκαρδία·
μοιχεῖαι·   δόλος·
ἐπιθυμίαι·   ὑπερηφανία·
πορνεῖαι·   κακία·
κλοπαί·   αὐθάδεια·
εἰδωλολατρίαι·   πλεονεξία·
μαγεῖαι·   αἰσχρολογία·
φαρμακίαι·   ζηλοτυπία·
(ἁρπαγαί·)   θρασύτης·
ψευδομαρτυρίαι·   ὕψος·
ὑποκρίσεις·   ἀλαζονεία·

5:2
διῶκται ἀγαθῶν·   οὐκ ἐλεοῦντες
μισοῦντες ἀλήθειαν·   πτωχόν·
ἀγαπῶντες ψεῦδος·   οὐ πονοῦντες
                                      ἐπὶ καταπονουμέμῳ·

οὐ γινώσκοντες   οὐ γινώσκοντες
   μισθὸν δικαιοσύνης·   τὸν ποιήσαντα αὐτούς·
οὐ κολλώμενοι ἀγαθῷ·
οὐδὲ κρίσει δικαίᾳ·   φονεῖς
                                      τέκνων·
                                   φθορεῖς
                                      πλάσματος θεοῦ·

ἀγρυπνοῦντες
   οὐκ εἰς τὸ ἀγαθόν·
   ἀλλ᾽ εἰς τὸ πονηρόν·   ἀποστρεφόμενοι
ὧν μακρὰν πραΰτης   τὸν ἐνδεόμενον·
   καὶ ὑπομονή·   καταπονοῦντες
μάταια ἀγαπῶντες·   τὸν θλιβόμενον·
διώκοντες ἀνταπόδομα·   πλουσίων παράκλητοι·
                                   πενήτων ἄνομοι κριταί·
                                   πανθαμαρτητοί·

ῥυσθείητε τέκνα ἀπὸ τούτων ἁπάντων.

5:1   The way of death, on_the_other_hand, is this:

first of all, it is evil and full of accursedness:

[A1] murders,
[A2] adulteries,
[A3] lusts,
[A4] illicit_sexual_acts,
[A5] thefts,
[A6] idolatries,
[A7] mägic,
[A8] potions,
[A9] sorceries, *robberies*
[A10] perjuries,
[A11] hypocrisies,

[A12] double-heartednesses,
[A13] trickery,
[A14] arrogance,
[A15] malice,
[A16] self-pleasing,
[A17] greed,
[A18] foul-speech,
[A19] jealousy,
[A20] audacity,
[A21] haughtiness,
[A22] false-pretension;

5:2

[B1] [those] persecutors of [the] good,
[B2] [those] hating [the] truth,
[B3] [those] loving lies,

[B4] [those] not knowing
   [the] wages of justice,
[B5] not associating with [the] good,
[B6] nor with just judgment,

[B7] [those] lying_awake [at night]
   not for good,
   but for wicked [things],
[B8] [those] far from being gentle
   and patient,
[B9] [those] loving frivolous [things],
[B10] [those] pursuing recompense
   [for everything they do],

[B11] [those] not showing_mercy
   to the poor,
[B12] not toiling for
   the one_weighed_down_by_
   toil,
[B13] [those] not knowing
   the one_having_made them,

[B14] [those] murderers of
   children,
[B15] [those] corruptors
   of God's workmanship

[B16] [those] turning away
   the needy,
[B17] [those] weighing_down_
   with toil the oppressed,
[B18] [those] advocates of the rich,
[B19] lawless judges of [the] poor,
[B20] [those] totally_sinful.

May ÿou be saved, [Oh] children, from all of these!

6:1   ὅρα μή τις σε πλανήσῃ
ἀπὸ ταύτης τῆς ὁδοῦ τῆς διδαχῆς·
ἐπεὶ παρεκτὸς θεοῦ σε διδάσκει·

6:2   εἰ μὲν γὰρ δύνασαι βαστάσαι ὅλον τὸν
ζυγὸν τοῦ κυρίου τέλειος ἔσῃ·
εἰ δ᾽ οὐ δύνασαι
ὃ δύνῃ τοῦτο ποίει·

6:3   περὶ δὲ τῆς βρώσεως·
ὃ δύνασαι βάστασον·
ἀπὸ δὲ τοῦ εἰδωλοθύτου
λίαν πρόσεχε·
λατπεία γάρ ἐστι θεῶν νεκρῶν·

7:1   περὶ δὲ τοῦ βαπτίσματος οὕτω βαπτίσατε·

ταῦτα πάντα προειπόντες βαπτίσατε·
εἰς τὸ ὄνομα τοῦ πατρὸς
καὶ τοῦ υἱοῦ
καὶ τοῦ ἁγίου πνεύματος
ἐν ὕδατι ζῶντι·

7:2   ἐὰν δὲ μὴ ἔχῃς ὕδωρ ζῶν·
εἰς ἄλλο ὕδωρ βάπτισον·
εἰ δ᾽ οὐ δύνασαι ἐν ψυχρῷ·
ἐν θερμῷ·
7:3   ἐὰν δὲ ἀμφότερα μὴ ἔχῃς·
ἔκχεον εἰς τὴν κεφαλὴν τρὶς ὕδωρ
εἰς ὄνομα πατρὸς
καὶ υἱοῦ
καῖ ἁγίου πνεύματος·

6:1   Look_out, lest anyone make you wander
from this way of training,
since without God he/she trains you.

6:2   [1] For, on_the_one_hand, if you are able to bear
the whole yoke of the Lord, you will be perfect;
[2] but if, on_the_other_hand, you are not able,
that which you are able, do this.   —— grace

6:3   (And) concerning eating,

Jewish Helburism

[1] bear that which you are able,
[2] from the food, on_the_other_hand, sacrificed to idols,
very_much keep_away,
for it is worship of dead gods.

7:1   (And) concerning baptism, bäptize thus:

Having said all these things beforehand,
ïmmerse in the name of the Father
and of the Son
and of the holy Spirit
in flowing water—

7:2   [1] if, on_the_other_hand, you should not have flowing water,
immerse in other water [that is available];
[2] (and) if you are not able in cold,   sorry Baptists
[immerse] in warm [water];

7:3   [3] (and) if you should not have either,
pour out water onto the head three times
in the name of [the] Father
and [the] Son
and [the] holy Spirit.

7:4   πρὸ δὲ τοῦ βαρτίσματος
       προνηστευσάτω ὁ βαπτίζων
       καὶ ὁ βαπτιζόμενος·
       καὶ εἴ τινες ἄλλοι δύνανται·

       κελεύεις δὲ νηστεῦσαι τὸν βαπτιζόμενον
       πρὸ μιᾶς ἢ δύο·

8:1   αἱ δὲ νηστεῖαι ὑμῶν·
       μὴ ἔστωσαν μετὰ τῶν ὑποκριτῶν·
           νηστεύουσι γὰρ δευτέρᾳ σαββάτων
               καὶ πέμπτῃ·
           ὑμεῖς δὲ νηστεύσατε τετράδα
               καὶ παρασκευήν·

8:2   μηδὲ προσεύχεσθε ὡς οἱ ὑποκριταί·
       ἀλλ᾽ ὡς ἐκέλευσεν ὁ κύριος ἐν τῷ εὐαγγελίῳ αὐτοῦ·

       οὕτως προσεύχεσθε·

           πάτερ ἡμῶν ὁ ἐν τῷ οὐρανῷ·
           ἁγιασθήτω τὸ ὄνομά σου·
           ἐλθέτω ἡ βασιλεία σου·
           γενηθήτω τὸ θέλημά σου·
           ὡς ἐν οὐρανῷ καὶ ἐπὶ γῆς·
           τὸν ἄρτον ἡμῶν τὸν ἐπιούσιον δὸς ἡμῖν σήμερον·
           καὶ ἄφες ἡμῖν τὴν ὀφειλὴν ἡμῶν·
               ὡς καὶ ἡμεῖς ἀφίεμεν τοῖς ὀφειλέταις ἡμῶν·
           καὶ μὴ εἰσενέγκῃς ἡμᾶς εἰς πειρασμόν·
               ἀλλὰ ῥῦσαι ἡμᾶς ἀπὸ τοῦ πονηροῦ·
           ὅτι σοῦ ἐστιν ἡ δύναμις καὶ ἡ δόξα εἰς τοὺς αἰῶνας·

8:3   τρὶς τῆς ἡμέρας οὕτω προσεύχεσθε·

7:4 (And) prior to the baptism,
[1] let the one_baptizing fast;
[2] and [let the] one_being_baptized;
[3] and if any others have_the_strength,
  [let them fast also].
Order, on_the_other_hand, the one_being_baptized to fast
during one or two [days] prior [to the baptism].

8:1 (And) lët ÿour fasts
not stand with the hypocrites,
  for they fast on the second
    and on the fifth [day] of the week
  ÿou fast, on_the_other_hand, during the fourth
    and during the [sabbath] preparation [day].

against Jewish fast schedules?

8:2 (And) dö not pray as the hypocrites
but as the Lord ordered in his good news.

Präy thus:

  Our Father, the [one] in heaven,
  your name be_made_holy,
  your kingdom come,
  your will be born upon earth as in heaven,
  give us this_day our loaf [that is] coming, *future aorist*
  and forgive us our debt [at the final judgment]
    as we likewise [now] forgive our debtors,
  and do not lead us into the trial [of the last days]
    but deliver us from [that] evil
  because yours is the power and the glory forever.

Very Gospel like almost word for word

8:3 Three times within the day präy thus.

9:1   περὶ δὲ τῆς εὐχαριστίας οὕτως εὐχαριστήσατε·

9:2   πρῶτον περὶ τοῦ ποτηρίου·

εὐχαριστοῦμέν σοι πάτερ ἡμῶν
ὑπὲρ τῆς ἁγίας ἀμπέλου δαυὶδ τοῦ παιδός σου·
ἧς ἐγνώρισας ἡμῖν διὰ ἰησοῦ τοῦ παιδός σου·
σοὶ ἡ δόξα εἰς τοὺς αἰῶνας·

9:3   περὶ δὲ τοῦ κλάσματος·

εὐχαριστοῦμέν σοι πάτερ ἡμῶν
ὑπὲρ τῆς ζωῆς καὶ γνώσεως
ἧς ἐγνώρισας ἡμῖν διὰ ἰησοῦ τοῦ παιδός σου·
σοὶ ἡ δόξα εἰς τοὺς αἰῶνας·

9:4   ὥσπερ ἦν τοῦτο <τὸ> κλάσμα διεσκορπισμένον
            ἐπάνω τῶν ὀρέων
        καὶ συναχθὲν ἐγένετο ἕν·
        οὕτω συναχθήτω σου ἡ ἐκκλησία
        ἀπὸ τῶν περάτων τῆς εἰς τὴν σὴν βασιλείαν·
        ὅτι σοῦ ἐστιν ἡ δόξα καὶ ἡ δύναμις
            διὰ ἰησοῦ χριστοῦ εἰς τοὺς αἰῶας·

9:5   μηδεὶς δὲ φαγέτω μηδὲ πιέτω ἀπὸ τῆς εὐχαριστίας ὑμῶν·
        ἀλλ᾽ οἱ βαπτισθέντες εἰς ὄνομα κυρίου·
            καὶ γὰρ περὶ τούτου εἴρηκεν ὁ κύριος·
            μὴ δῶτε τὸ ἅγιον τοῖς κυσί·

9:1   (And) concerning the eucharist, ëucharistize thus:

9:2   First, concerning the cup:

Revise order

We give you thanks, our Father,
for the holy vine of your servant David
which you revealed to us through your servant Jesus.
To you [is] the glory forever.

4 cups of wine during passover ceremony

9:3   And concerning the broken [loaf]:

We give you thanks, our Father,
for the life and knowledge
which you revealed to us through your servant Jesus.
To you [is] the glory forever.

Take, broke, blessed, gave

9:4   Just as this broken [loaf] was scattered
      over the hills [as grain],
and, having_been_gathered_together, became one;
in_like_fashion, may your church be_gathered_together
from the ends of the earth into your kingdom.
Because yours is the glory and the power
      through Jesus Christ forever.

Feeding of 5000, 4000

Eugene Peterson "Christ plays in Ten thousand places"

9:5   (And) lët no one eat or drink from ÿour eucharist
      except those baptized in the name of [the] Lord,
            for the Lord has likewise said concerning this:
            "Do not give what is holy to the dogs."

10:1   μετὰ δὲ τὸ ἐμπλησθῆναι οὕτως εὐχαριστήσατε·

10:2   εὐχαριστοῦμέν σοι πάτερ ἅγιε
ὑπὲρ τοῦ ἁγίου ὀνόματός σου
οὗ κατεσκήνωσας ἐν ταῖς καρδίαις ἡμῶν·
καὶ ὑπὲρ τῆς γνώσεως καὶ πίστεως καὶ ἀθανασίας·
ἧς ἐγνώρισας ἡμῖν διὰ ἰησοῦ τοῦ παιδός σου <·>
σοὶ ἡ δόξα εἰς τοὺς αἰῶνας·

10:3   σύ δέσποτα παντοκράτορ ἔκτισας τὰ πάντα
ἕνεκεν τοῦ ὀνόματός σου·
τροφήν τε καὶ ποτὸν ἔδωκας τοῖς ἀνθρώπων εἰς ἀπόλαυσιν·
ἵνα σοι εὐχαριστήσωσιν·
ἡμῖν δὲ ἐχαρίσω
πνευματικὴν τροφὴν καὶ ποτὸν καὶ ζωὴν αἰώνιον
διὰ τοῦ παιδός σου·

10:4   πρὸ πάντων εὐχαριστοῦμέν σοι
ὅτι δυνατὸς εἶ σὺ <·>
<σοὶ> ἡ δόξα εἰς τοὺς αἰῶνας·

10:5   μνήσθητι κύριε τῆς ἐκκλησίας σου
τοῦ ῥύσασθαι αὐτὴν ἀπὸ παντὸς πονηροῦ·
καὶ τελειῶσαι αὐτὴν ἐν τῇ ἀγάπῃ σου·
καὶ σύναξον αὐτὴν ἀπὸ τῶν τεσσάρων ἀνέμων·
τὴν ἁγιασθεῖσαν εἰς τὴν σὴν βασιλείαν·
ἣν ἡτοίμασας αὐτῇ·
ὅτι σοῦ ἐστιν ἡ δύναμις καὶ ἡ δόξα εἰς τοὺς αἰῶνας·

10:6   ἐλθέτω χάρις
καὶ παρελθέτω ὁ κόσμος οὗτος·
ὡσαννὰ τῷ θεῷ δαυΐδ·
Εἴ τις ἅγιός ἐστιν ἐρχέσθω·
εἴ τις οὐκ ἔστι μετανοείτω·
μαραναθά ἀμήν·

10:7   τοῖς δὲ προφήταις ἐπιτρέπετε
εὐχαριστεῖν ὅσα θέλουσιν·

10:1   And after being filled [by the meal], ëucharistize thus:

10:2   We give you thanks, holy Father,
       for your holy name,
       which you tabernacle in our hearts,
       and for the knowledge and faith and immortality
       which you revealed to us through your servant Jesus.
       To you [is] the glory forever.

10:3   You, almighty Master, created all things
       for the sake of your name,
       both food and drink you have given to people for enjoyment
       in order that they might give thanks;
       to us, on_the_other_hand, you have graciously_bestowed
       Spirit-sent food and drink for life forever
              through your servant [Jesus].

10:4   Before all [these] things, we give you thanks
       because you are powerful [on our behalf].
       To you [is] the glory forever.

10:5   Remember, Lord, your church,
              to save [her] from every evil
              and to perfect [her] in your love
              and to gather [her] together from the four winds
       [as] the sanctified into your kingdom
       which you have prepared for her,
       because yours is the power and the glory forever.

Bread scattered regathered

10:6   [A] Come, grace [of the kingdom]!
              and pass_away, [Oh] this world!
       [B] Hosanna to the God of David!
       [C] If anyone is holy, come!
              If anyone is not, convert!
       [D] Come Lord [maran atha]! Amen!

Jesus aramaic

10:7   (And) türn toward the prophets [allowing them]
       to eucharistize as much as they wish.

11:1   ὅς ἂν οὖν ἐλθὼν διδάξῃ ὑμᾶς ταῦτα πάντα τὰ προειρημένα

        δέξασθε αὐτόν·
11:2   ἐὰν δὲ αὐτὸς ὁ διδάσκων
        στραφεὶς
        διδάσκῃ ἄλλην διδαχήν
        εἰς τὸ καταλῦσαι·
          μὴ αὐτοῦ ἀκούσητε·
        εἰς δὲ τὸ προσθεῖναι δικαιοσύνην
          καὶ γνῶσιν κυρίου·
          δέξασθε αὐτὸν ὡς κύριον·

11:3   περὶ δὲ τῶν ἀποστόλων καὶ προφητῶν
        κατὰ τὸ δόγμα τοῦ εὐαγγελίου·
        οὕτως ποιήσατε·

11:4   πᾶς δὲ ἀπόστολος ἐρχόμενος πρὸς
        ὑμᾶς δεχθήτω ὡς κύριος·
11:5   οὐ μενεῖ δὲ <εἰ μὴ> ἡμέραν μίαν·

        ἐὰν δὲ ᾖ χρεία καὶ τὴν ἄλλην·
        τρεῖς δὲ ἐὰν μείνῃ
          ψευδοπροφήτης ἐστίν·
11:6   ἐξερχόμενος δὲ
        ὁ ἀπόστολος μηδὲν λαμβανέτω·
          εἰ μὴ ἄρτον
          ἕως οὗ αὐλισθῇ·
        ἐὰν δὲ ἀργύριον αἰτῇ
          ψευδοπροφήτης ἐστί·

11:1   [A] Whoever, then, should train ÿou in all these things said
                   beforehand,
               rëceive him/her.
11:2   [B] If, on_the_other_hand, the one training,
               him/herself having been turned around,
               should train [ÿou] in another tradition
               [1] for the destroying [of things said beforehand],
                   dö not listen to him/her;
               [2] but, [if it is] for the supplementing of justice
                   and knowledge of [the] Lord,
                   rëceive him/her as [the] Lord!

11:3   And concerning the apostle-prophets,
           in_accordance_with the decree of the good news,
           äct thus:

11:4   [A] (And) every apostle coming to ÿou,
               lët [him/her] be received as [the] Lord:
11:5   [1] he/she will not remain, on_the_other_hand, except one
                       day;
               [2] (and) if ever there be need, also another [day];
               [3] (but) if ever he/she should remain three [days],
                   he/she is a false prophet.
11:6   [B] (And), going_out,
               [1] lët the apostle take nothing except a loaf
                   [that he/she needs to tide him/her over]
                   until he/she might lodge [in another courtyard],
               [2] if, on_the_other_hand, he/she should ask for silver,
                   he/she is a false prophet.

Compare
to Ignatius'
letters. Deeds
not just Doctrine

11:7   καὶ πάντα προφήτην λαλοῦντα ἐν πνεύματι,
         οὐ πειράσετε· οὐδὲ διακρινεῖτε·
         πᾶσα γὰρ ἁμαρτία ἀφεθήσεται·
         αὕτη δὲ ἡ ἁμαρτία οὐκ ἀφεθήσεται·
11:8   οὐ πᾶς δὲ ὁ λαλῶν ἐν πνεύματι προφήτης ἐστίν·
         ἀλλ᾽ ἐὰν ἔχῃ τοὺς τρόπους κυρίου·

         ἀπὸ οὖν τῶν τρόπων γνωσθήσεται
         ὁ ψευδοφροφήτης καὶ ὁ προφήτης·

11:9   καὶ πᾶς προφήτης ὁρίζων τράπεζαν ἐν πνεύματι,

         οὐ φάγεται ἀπ᾽ αὐτῆς·
         εἰ δὲ μήγε ψευδοπροφήτης ἐστίν·
11:10   πᾶς δὲ προφήτης διδάσκων τὴν ἀλήθειαν
         εἰ ἃ διδάσκει οὐ ποιεῖ
         ψευδοπροφήτης ἐστίν·
11:11   πᾶς δὲ προφήτης δεδοκιμασμένος ἀληθινός

         ποιῶν εἰς μυστήριον κοσμικὸν ἐκκλησίας·
         μὴ διδάσκων δὲ ποιεῖν ὅσα αὐτὸς ποιεῖ

         οὐ κριθήσεται ἐφ᾽ ὑμῶν·
         μετὰ θεοῦ γὰρ ἔχει τὴν κρίσιν·
         ὡσαύτως γὰρ ἐποίησαν καὶ οἱ ἀρχαῖοι προφῆται·
11:12   ὅς δ᾽ ἂν εἴπῃ ἐν πνεύματι
         δός μοι ἀργύρια ἢ ἕτερά τινα
         οὐκ ἀκούσεσθε αὐτοῦ·
         ἐὰν δὲ περὶ ἄλλων ὑστερούντων
         εἴπῃ δοῦναι
         μηδεὶς αὐτὸν κρινέτω·

11:7   [A] And every prophet speaking in Spirit
    ÿou should not put_on_trial and not judge;
      for every sin will be forgiven
      but this sin will not be forgiven.

11:8   [B] (But) not everyone speaking in Spirit is a prophet,
    but if [he/she is], he/she should have the habits of [the]
      Lord.
    Therefore, from these habits should be known
    the false_prophet and the [true] prophet.

[handwritten margin notes: pro before / pous - foot / walkin the steps of Christ ?]

11:9   [A] And every prophet ordering a dining-table [to be set] in
      Spirit
    will not eat from it, (and) if [he/she acts] otherwise,
      he/she is really a false_prophet.

[handwritten margin note: eat what you expect others to eat]

11:10 [B] (And) every prophet teaching the truth,
    if he/she does not do what he/she teaches,
      he/she is a false prophet.

11:11 [C] (And) every prophet having been put to the test [and found
      to be] true,
    doing a (worldly mystery of the church,)
    (but) not training [ÿou] to do what he himself [/she herself]
      does,
    he/she will not be judged by ÿou;
      for with God he/she has his/her judgment;
      for just so acted also the ancient prophets.

[handwritten margin note: Heavenly minded / no earthly Good]

11:12 [D] (But) whoever [in this category] should say in Spirit,
    [1] "Give me silver or any_other thing,"
      ÿou will not listen to him/her;
    [2] (but) if, concerning others being in want,
      he/she should say to give,
      lët no one judge him/her.

12:1   πᾶς δὲ ὁ ἐρχόμενος ἐν ὀνόματι κυρίου·
        δεχθήτω·
        ἔπειτα δὲ δοκιμάσαντες αὐτὸν·
        γνώσεσθε·
        σύνεσιν γὰρ ἕξετε δεξιὰν καὶ ἀριστεράν·

12:2   εἰ μὲν παρόδιός ἐστιν ὁ ἐρχόμενος
        βοηθεῖτε αὐτῷ ὅσον δύνασθε·
        οὐ μενεῖ δὲ πρὸς ὑμᾶς
            εἰ μὴ δύο ἢ τρεῖς ἡμέρας·
            ἐὰν ᾖ ἀνάγκη·
12:3   εἰ δὲ θέλει πρὸς ὑμᾶς καθῆσθαι

        τεχνίτης ὢν ἐργαζέσθω καὶ φαγέτω·
12:4   εἰ δὲ οὐκ ἔχει τέχνην·
        κατὰ τὴν σύνεσιν ὑμῶν προνοήσατε·
        πῶς μὴ ἀργὸς μεθ᾽ ὑμῶν ζήσεται χριστιανός·
12:5   εἰ δ᾽ οὐ θέλει οὕτω ποιεῖν
        χριστέμπορός ἐστιν·
        προσέχετε ἀπὸ τῶν τοιούτων·

12:1   (And), everyone coming in [the] name of [the] Lord,
        lët [him] be received;
    (and) thereafter, having put him/her to the test,
        ÿou will know,
        for ÿou will have understanding [of] right and left.

12:2   [A] If, on_the_one_hand, the one coming is a traveler,
        [1] hëlp him/her, as much as ÿou are able;
        [2] he/she will not remain, on_the_other_hand, among ÿou,
            except for two or three days,
            if ever there should be a necessity.

12:3   [B] If, on_the_other_hand, he/she wishes to settle down
            among ÿou,
        being a craftsman, let him/her work and let him/her eat.

12:4   [C] If, on_the_other_hand, he/she does not have a craft,
        according to ÿour understanding, plän beforehand
        how a Christian will live among ÿou, not [being] idle.

12:5   [D] If, on_the_other_hand, he/she does not wish to act thus,
        he/she is a Christ-peddler.
        Bëware of such ones!

13:1   πᾶς δὲ προφήτης ἀληθινός θέλων καθῆσθαι πρὸς ὑμᾶς·

        ἄξιός ἐστιν τῆς τροφῆς αὐτοῦ
13:2   ὡσαύτως διδάσκαλος ἀληθινός ἐστιν ἄξιος καὶ αὐτὸς
        ὥσπερ ὁ ἐργάτης τῆς τροφῆς αὐτοῦ·

13:3   πᾶσαν οὖν ἀπαρχὴν γεννημάτων
            ληνοῦ καὶ ἄλωνος·
            βοῶν τε καὶ προβάτων λαβὼν·
            δώσεις τὴν ἀπαρχὴν τοῖς προφήταις·
            αὐτοὶ γάρ εἰσιν οἱ ἀρχιερεῖς ὑμῶν·

13:4   ἐὰν δὲ μὴ ἔχητε προφήτην
            δότε τοῖς πτωχοῖς·

13:5   ἐὰν σιτίαν ποιῇς
            τὴν ἀπαρχὴν λαβὼν
            δὸς κατὰ τὴν ἐντολήν·
13:6   ὡσαύτως κεράμιον οἴνου ἢ ἐλαίου ἀνοίξας
            τὴν ἀπαρχὴν λαβὼν
            δὸς τοῖς προφήταις·
13:7   ἀργυρίου δὲ καὶ ἱματισμοῦ καὶ παντὸς
            κτήματος λαβὼν τὴν ἀπαρχήν·
            ὡς ἄν σοι δόξῃ
            δὸς κατὰ τὴν ἐντολήν·

13:1   [A] (And) every true prophet wishing to settle down among
           ÿou
       is worthy of his/her food;
13:2   [B] a true teacher is worthy likewise,
           just as the laborer, of his/her food.

13:3   [A] So, every first_fruits of the products
               of the wine_vat and threshing_floor,
               of both cattle and sheep,
           [1] you will give the first_fruits to the prophets;
               for they themselves are your high-priests.

13:4   [2] (But) if ÿou should not have a prophet,
               gïve [it] to the beggars.

13:5   [B] If you should make bread-dough,
           taking the first_fruits,
           give according to the rule.
13:6   [C] Similarly, having opened a jar of wine or of oil,
           taking the first_fruits,
           give to the prophets.
13:7   [D] (And) of silver and of clothing and of every possession,
           taking the first_fruits,
           as it might_seem_appropriate to you,
           give according to the rule.

14:1   κατά κυριακὴν δὲ κυρίου

    συναχθέντες κλάσατε ἄρτον·
    καὶ εὐχαριστήσατε προσεξομολογησάμενοι
    τὰ παραπτώματα ὑμῶν·
      ὅπως καθαρὰ ἡ θυσία ὑμῶν ᾖ·

14:2   πᾶς δὲ ἔχων τὴν ἀμφιβολίαν μετὰ τοῦ ἑταίρου αὐτοῦ

    μὴ συνελθέτω ὑμῖν
    ἕως οὗ διαλλαγῶσιν·
      ἵνα μὴ κοινωθῇ ἡ θυσία ὑμῶν·

14:3   αὕτη γάρ ἐστιν ἡ ῥηθεῖσα ὑπὸ κυρίου < >
    ἐν παντὶ τόπῳ καὶ χρόνῳ προσφέρειν μοι θυσίαν καθαράν·
    ὅτι βασιλεὺς μέγας εἰμί λέγει κύριος·
    καὶ τὸ ὄνομά μου θαυμαστὸν ἐν τοῖς ἔθνεσι.

15:1   χειροτονήσατε οὖν ἑαυτοῖς
      ἐπισκόπους καὶ διακόνους ἀξίους τοῦ κυρίου
    ἄνδρας πραεῖς
    καὶ ἀφιλαργύρους
    καὶ ἀληθεῖς
    καὶ δεδοκιμασμένους·
      ὑμῖν γὰρ λειτουργοῦσι καὶ αὐτοὶ
      τὴν λειτουργίαν
      τῶν προφητῶν καὶ διδασκάλων·

15:2   μὴ οὖν ὑπερίδητε αὐτούς·
    αὐτοὶ γάρ εἰσιν οἱ τετιμημένοι ὑμῶν·
    μετὰ τῶν προφητῶν καὶ διδασκάλων·

15:3   ἐλέγχετε δὲ ἀλλήλους. μὴ ἐν ὀργῇ· ἀλλ᾽ ἐν εἰρήνῃ·
    ὡς ἔχετε ἐν τῷ εὐαγγελίῳ·
    καὶ παντὶ ἀστοχοῦντι κατὰ τοῦ ἑτέρου
    μηδεὶς λαλείτω·
    μηδὲ παρ᾽ ὑμῶν ἀκουέτω·
      ἕως οὗ μετανοήσῃ·

15:4   τὰς δὲ εὐχὰς ὑμῶν καὶ τὰς ἐλεημοσύνας καὶ πάσας τὰς πράξεις·
    οὕτως ποιήσατε ὡς ἔχετε ἐν τῷ εὐαγγελίῳ τοῦ κυρίου ἡμῶν·

14:1   (And) according to [the] divinely_instituted [day/rule] of [the]
            Lord,
        having_been_gathered_together, brëak a loaf.
        [A] And ëucharistize, having_beforehand_confessed
                ÿour failings,
            so_that ÿour sacrifice may be pure.

14:2   [B] Everyone, on_the_other_hand, having a conflict with a
                companion,
            dö not let [him/her] come_together with ÿou
            until they_have_been_reconciled,
                in_order_that ÿour sacrifice may not be defiled.

14:3   For this is [the thing] having_been_said by [the] Lord:
            "In every place and time, offer to me a pure sacrifice.
            "Because a great king am I," says [the] Lord,
            "and my name [is] wondrous among the gentiles."

15:1   [A] Appöint, then, for ÿourselves,
                bishop and deacons worthy of the Lord,
            [1] men gentle
            [2] and not_money-loving
            [3] and truthful
            [4] and tested;
                for to ÿou they likewise serve (unpaid)
                the unpaid_public_service
                of the prophet-teachers.

15:2   [B] Dö not, then, look down upon them;
                for they themselves are your honored ones
                with the prophet-teachers.

15:3   [A] (And) rëprove each other not in anger, but in peace,
                as ÿou have [it] in the good news.
        [B] And to everyone misbehaving against the other,
                [1] lët no one speak [to him/her]
                [2] nor hear from ÿou [about him/her]
                    until he/she should repent.

15:4   (And) ÿour prayers and alms and all [ÿour] actions
        dö thus as ÿou have [it] in the good news of our Lord.

16:1   γρηγορεῖτε ὑπὲρ τῆς ζωῆς ὑμῶν·
οἱ λύχνοι ὑμῶνμὴ σβεσθήτωσαν·
καὶ αἱ ὀσφύες ὑμῶν μὴ ἐκλυέσθωσαν·
ἀλλὰ γίνεσθε ἕτοιμοι·
οὐ γὰρ οἴδατε τὴν ὥραν ἐν ᾗ ὁ κύριος ἡμῶν ἔρχεται·

16:2   πυκνῶς δὲ συναχθήσεσθε
ζητοῦντες τὰ ἀνήκοντα ταῖς ψυχαῖς ὑμῶν·
οὐ γὰρ ὠφελήσει ὑμᾶς ὁ πᾶς χρόνος τῆς πίστεως ὑμῶν
ἐὰν μὴ ἐν τῷ ἐσχάτῳ καιρῷ τελειωθῆτε·
16:3   ἐν γάρ ταῖς ἐσχάταις ἡμέραις
πληθυνθήσονται οἱ ψευδοπροφῆται καὶ οἱ φθορεῖς·
καὶ στραφήσονται τὰ πρόβατα εἰς λύκους·
καὶ ἡ ἀγάπη στραφήσεται εἰς μῖσος·
16:4   αὐξανούσης γὰρ τῆς ἀνομίας,
μισήσουσιν ἀλλήλους
καὶ διώξουσιν
καὶ παραδώσουσι·
καὶ τότε φανήσεται ὁ κοσμοπλανὴς ὡς υἱὸς θεοῦ·
καὶ ποιήσει σημεῖα καὶ τέρατα·
καὶ ἡ γῆ παραδοθήσεται εἰς χεῖρας αὐτοῦ·
καὶ ποιήσει ἀθέμιτα
ἃ οὐδέποτε γέγονεν ἐξ αἰῶνος·
16:5   τότε ἥξει ἡ κτίσις τῶν ἀνθρώπων
εἰς τὴν πύρωσιν τῆς δοκιμασίας·
καὶ σκανδαλισθήσονται πολλοὶ καὶ ἀπολοῦνται·

οἱ δὲ ὑπομείναντες ἐν τῇ πίστει αὐτῶν

σωθήσονται ὑπ᾽ αὐτοῦ τοῦ καταθέματος·
16:6   καὶ τότε φανήσεται τὰ σημεῖα τῆς ἀληθείας·
πρῶτον· σημεῖον ἐκπετάσεως ἐν οὐρανῷ·
εἶτα σημεῖον φωνῆς σάλπιγγος·
καὶ τὸ τρίτον ἀνάστασις νεκρῶν·
16:7   οὐ πάντων δέ·
ἀλλ᾽ ὡς ἐρρέθη·
ἥξει ὁ κύριος καὶ πάντες οἱ ἅγιοι μετ᾽ αὐτοῦ·
16:8   τότε ὄψεται ὁ κόσμος τὸν κύριον ἐρχόμενον
ἐπάνω τῶν νεφελῶν τοῦ οὐρανοῦ.

16:1   [A] Bë_watchful over ÿour life;
             [1] do not let ÿour lamps be_quenched,
             [2] and do not let ÿour loins be_let_loose.
        [B] But bë prepared;
             for ÿou do not know the hour in which our Lord is coming.

16:2   [C] (And) frequently bë_gathered_together,
             seeking the things pertaining to ÿour souls;
                  for the whole time of ÿour faith will not be of use to ÿou
                  if in the end time ÿou should not have been perfected.
16:3   [1] For, in the last days,
             [a] the false_prophets and the corrupters will be multiplied,
             [b] and the sheep will be turned into wolves,
             [c] and the love will be turned into hate.
16:4   For, with lawlessness increasing,
                  [a] they will hate each other
                  [b] and they will persecute
                  [c] and they will betray [the love].
        [2] And then will appear the world-deceiver as a son of God,
             [a] and he will do signs and wonders,
             [b] and the earth will be betrayed into his hands,
             [c] and he will do unlawful things
                  that never have happened from the beginning of time.
16:5   [3] Then the creation of humans will come
             into the burning-process of testing,
             [a] and many will be entrapped and will be utterly_
                  destroyed,
             [b] the ones having remained firm in their faith, on_the_
                  other_hand,
                  will be saved by the accursed [burning-process] itself.
16:6   [4] And then will appear the signs of the truth:
             [a] [the] first sign [will be the] unfurling [banner] in heaven,
             [b] next [the] sign of [the] sound of [the] trumpet,
             [c] and the third [sign will be the] resurrection of [the] dead—
16:7   not [the resurrection] of all, on_the_other_hand,
                  but as it has been said:
                  "The Lord will come and all the holy_ones with him."
16:8   [5] Then the world will see the Lord coming
             atop the clouds of heaven.

A Brief Commentary[1]

Any community that cannot artfully and effectively pass on its cherished way of life as a program for divine wisdom and graced existence cannot long endure. Any way of life that cannot be clearly specified, exhibited, and differentiated from the alternative modes operative within the surrounding culture is doomed to growing insignificance and gradual assimilation. Faced with these harsh realities, the *Didache* unfolds the training program calculated to irreversibly alter the habits of perception and standards of judgment of novices coming out of a pagan lifestyle. The content and modality of this process of human transformation can be gleaned from the verbal clues conveyed within the text itself. The task of this commentary is to begin to unravel these clues and to recover the passion, the content, and the methodology with which those proponents of the Jesus movement associated with the *Didache* set out to form and transform the lives of gentiles into that graced perfection demanded for ready inclusion into the anticipated Kingdom of God on earth.

The *Didache* holds the secret of how and why Jesus of Nazareth, a seemingly insignificant Galilean Jew executed as a Roman criminal, went on to attract and convert the world. Sure enough, the members of the Jesus movement regarded him as both "Son of God" and "Son of David" who had been sent by the Father to prepare the world for his coming kingdom. In fairness, however, such exalted claims were a

[1] This brief commentary is neither exhaustive nor definitive. Having just completed a thousand-page commentary (Milavec 2003) painstakingly assembled over a period of fifteen years, I realize that here I can only mark out some of the salient contours of the text and expose a few facets of the lived experience it presupposes. At this juncture, however, this will suffice. My purpose is to generate interest and to open up lines of inquiry that readers will pursue in their own way and at their own leisure.

commonplace within the religious flux of the Roman Empire (see, e.g., Crossan 1994:1–28) and, at first glance, barely caused a ripple in the day-to-day business of deciding which of the many religious systems was worthy of personal adherence. In truth, potential members assessed the movement not so much on the basis of claims made on behalf of Jesus who was absent, but on the basis of their experience of the way of life of members who were very much present to them. It is no surprise, therefore, that the entire system of the *Didache* displays little taste for negotiating, defining, and defending the exalted titles and functions of Jesus. Rather, the *Didache* is taken up with the business of passing on the Way of Life revealed to its authors by the Father through his servant Jesus. Converts came forward ready to assimilate that Way of Life as it was formulated and lived out by the tried and tested members of the movement.

Whether "the Twelve" Authored the *Didache*

The sole complete manuscript of the *Didache* that has come down to us was discovered in 1873 by Archbishop Bryennios in the library of the Jerusalem Monastery of the Most Holy Sepulchre in Istanbul. The manuscript itself has two titles. The first and short title is *Training of the Twelve Disciples*. The second and long title is *Training of the Lord through the Twelve Apostles to the Gentiles*. Since both the short and long titles begin with the Greek word *Didachē* ("Training"), scholars use the first word of both titles as a shorthand reference to the entire work. Moreover, in English translation scholars have rendered *didachē* as "teaching" rather than "training." My preference for "training" will be explained shortly.

The two titles (#1a)[2] found at the beginning of the eleventh-century manuscript cannot be presumed to be those in use during the first cen-

---

[2] Throughout this commentary I have made judgments regarding the many alternative opinions held by other scholars. In order to glimpse the interior logic and progression of topics in the text itself I have eliminated this technical discussion. As I go forward, however, I have listed the cross-references (#4c = Chapter Four, box c) to the specialized material found within the four hundred boxes in my thousand-page commentary (Milavec 2003). Interested persons who wish to pursue (a) information on the social, religious, and historical background of the first century and (b) scholarly opinions on disputed aspects of the *Didache* are invited to consult the boxes in this larger commentary.

tury. The *Didache* clearly offers internal evidence that it presents "training" (1:3) given by "the Lord" (9:3); whether this was transmitted by the "twelve apostles," however, is problematic. Apart from the titles the *Didache* itself never mentions "twelve" apostles. More importantly, when the subject of "apostles" does come up, this title was applied to charismatics passing through the community (11:3-6). If these "apostles" were indeed the Twelve, it remains difficult to understand why their stay would be limited to one or two days (11:5), why some of them would be inappropriately asking for silver (11:6), why some of them would be tearing down the received tradition (11:2). The "apostles" familiar to the framers of the *Didache*, therefore, were neither the Twelve nor the founders of the Didache communities. The distinct possibility remains, therefore, that "the Twelve Apostles" was deliberately introduced only at the point when apostolic authorship was recognized as an absolute necessity for any work seeking inclusion in the canon of approved books. Thus authorship cannot be decided on the basis of the received titles.

Therefore the *Didache* needs to be regarded as an anonymous document. As with so many books in the Christian Scriptures, one must allow for the probability that it did not originate with a single individual. Furthermore, given the manifest clues of orality[3] within the *Didache*

---

[3] Within the *Didache* the vocabulary and linguistic structure display a one-sided preference for orality. Thus the *Didache* defines the Way of Life and immediately goes on to specify the "training" required for the assimilation "of these *words*" (1:3). The novice is told to honor "the one *speaking* to you the *word* of God" (4:1), signaling that oral training was presupposed. Moreover, the novice trembles "at the *words* that you have *heard*" (3:8). In every instance where the *Didache* cites specific mandates from the Hebrew Scriptures the oral aspect (as opposed to the written) is highlighted: "It has been *said*" (1:6); "The Lord has likewise *said*" (9:5); "This is the thing having been *said* by the Lord" (14:3); "As it has been *said*" (16:7). The same thing can be presumed to hold true when citing the "good news" (8:2; 11:3; 15:3, 4; see #11e). Accordingly the *Didache* gives full attention to speaking rightly (1:3b; 2:3, 5; 4:8b, 14; 15:3b) and says nothing of false or empty writing. At baptism the novice is immersed in water, "having *said* all these things beforehand" (7:1). Thus when the novice is warned to watch out for those who "might make you wander from this way of training" (6:1) one surmises that defective words rather than defective texts are implied. The same holds true when, later in the *Didache*, the baptized are warned only to receive him/her who "should train you in all the things *said* beforehand" (11:1), indicating that even the *Didache* was being heard. Finally, faced with the end-time, each one is alerted to the importance of frequently being "gathered together" (16:2). This enforces an earlier admonition to "seek every day the presence of the

itself, one can be quite certain that it was originally composed orally and that it belonged to an extended network of persons who cherished and preserved it because it served to specify the standards of excellence guiding their Way of Life. Within a society based upon oral memory,[4] therefore, one must allow that the *Didache* might have circulated for a good many years before any occasion arose to prepare a textual version.

Division and Progression of Topics

The *Didache* does not have a topic paragraph serving to specify its overall purpose and name the progression of topics to be treated. Nonetheless, the framers of the *Didache* did make ample use of topic sentences (or phrases) to signal the beginning of new sections. In addition, the author used summary statements (4:14b, 13:1-2, 15:4) and final cautions (4:12-14a, 6:1-2, 11:1-2) in order to bring closure to blocks of material before passing on to the next topic. When attention is given to these linguistic clues the *Didache* breaks down into five topical divi-

---

saints in order that you may rest upon their *words*" (4:2)—thereby signaling once again how verbal exchange was paramount when "seeking the things pertaining to your souls" (16:2). The one misbehaving, accordingly, was reproved "not in anger [i.e., angry words], but in peace" (15:3). Those unable to abide by the reproof received were cut off from hearing or being discussed by community members: "Let no one *speak* to him/her, nor *hear* from you about him/her until he/she should repent" (15:3).

From beginning to end, therefore, the vocabulary and linguistic structure of the *Didache* reinforce oral performance. The literary world of seeing, reading, writing, and editing are entirely passed over in silence (Henderson 1992:295–99). This feature has repercussions as to how the *Didache* was created, transmitted, interpreted, and transformed in "a culture of high residual orality which nevertheless communicated significantly by means of literary creations" (Achtemeier 1990:9–19, 26–27).

[4] Given the literary bias of our present culture it is difficult to imagine how the *Didache* might have been created in "a culture of high residual orality" (Achtemeier 1990:3) wherein "oral sources" (attached to respected persons) were routinely given greater weight and were immeasurably more serviceable than "written sources" (Achtemeier 1990:9–11; Ong 1967:52–53). Since the vocabulary and linguistic structure of the *Didache* reinforce oral performance, the literary world of seeing, reading, writing, and editing present inadequate categories for appreciating the *Didache* (Henderson 1992:295–99; Milavec 2003:715–23). If the *Didache* is fundamentally oral in character, it ought to be heard. (See the section on electronic aids in the Bibliography.)

sions. Each of these divisions occupies progressively smaller fractions of the entire text, as shown by the numbers in parentheses:

   I. Training Program in the Way of Life (44%) *Did*. 1:1–6:2

  II. Regulations for Eating, Baptizing, Fasting, Praying (22%) *Did*. 6:3–11:2

 III. Regulations for Hospitality/Testing Various Classes of Visitors (15%) *Did*. 11:3–13:2

  IV. Regulations for First Fruits and for Offering a Pure Sacrifice (10%) *Did*. 13:3–15:4

   V. Closing Apocalyptic Forewarnings and Hope (9%) *Did*. 16:1-8

Each of these five subdivisions has enough internal coherence to stand alone. When placed together in their given order, however, they reveal a deliberate progression. Part I provides a detailed outline of how new members are to be initiated into the Way of Life prior to their baptism, while Part II details the regulations for eating, fasting, and praying after baptism. Part II looks backward to Part I and forward to Part III. Thus early in Part II baptism includes "having said all these things beforehand" (7:1)—a looking backward to the training (1:3) that occupies Part I. Part II ends with a caution to preserve "all these things said beforehand" against unnamed visitors who might "train you in another tradition" (11:2)—a looking forward to the potentially troublesome classes of visitors treated in Part III. Part III, in its turn, ends with the note that tested and true prophets "wishing to settle down among you" are "worthy of food" (13:1)—thereby looking forward to Part IV, which treats of the rules regarding first fruits. Part IV looks backward to Part III insofar as first fruits are preferentially given to approved "prophets" (13:3). Then regulations treating the pure sacrifice are given that look backward to the eucharist (9:1–10:7) in Part II and the training to confess one's failings (4:14) in Part I. Part IV, in sum, looks backward to the first three parts of the *Didache*.

Part V, at first glance, might appear to be an apocalyptic discourse that was tacked on to a unified instruction in four parts. When examined in detail, however, this discourse evokes a sense of urgency to "frequently be gathered together" (16:2)—a theme implied in the first three parts (4:2; 9:1–10:7; 14:1-2). Likewise the scenario of the end times gives first place to the ungodly work of "false prophets and corruptors" (16:3)—an echo of warnings already given in the first three parts (6:1; 11:1-2; 11:3–12:1). Finally, the closing discourse warns that "the whole time of your faith will not be of use to you if in the last time you should not have been perfected" (16:2)—a looking backward to the training in the Way of Life in Part I that closes saying, "If you are able to bear the whole yoke of the Lord [as just detailed], you will be perfect" (6:2). In effect, Part V is not a chance appendix but would appear to be deliberately crafted to advance the agenda of the first three parts of the *Didache*.

The Opening Definitions of the Way of Life

The opening line of the *Didache* serves as a topic sentence: "There are two ways: one of life, the other of death" (1:1). The Way of Life is defined immediately (1:2), but one has to pass through four chapters before the Way of Death is finally defined (5:1-2). The framers did not use these definitions in order to confront their hearers/readers with an existential choice between the Way of Life and the Way of Death. Rather, they pulled these two definitions apart in order to linguistically frame their main attraction, that is, the training program that occupies the central eight-tenths of Part I. The training program itself is introduced with a fresh topic sentence (1:3a) and closes with a summary statement (4:14b). This second framing device reinforces the centrality of the training program and again demonstrates that the definitions of the Two Ways have only a subsidiary interest for the author.

The rhetorical shifts in Part I of the *Didache* confirm this emphasis. The text opens with the Way of Life being described in the present indicative. The tone is descriptive. As soon as "the training" begins, however, the text shifts into the imperative. Concrete demands are being made. The mentor directly addresses the one being trained. Given the oral character of the *Didache* (#11d) and the prevalence of mnemonic aids, one can surmise that the spiritual guide had the entire Two Ways committed to memory. Within this section, therefore, one "overhears" the oral template of the "word of God" (4:1) used by the spiritual master. As soon as "the training" is finished, the text returns to the indicative in order to take up the description of the Way of Death (5:1f). Seen as a whole, Part I may be visualized as follows: the two definitions (in the present indicative) frame the central training program (in the present imperative and future indicative):

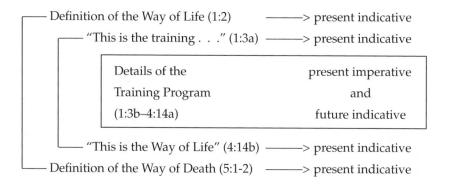

The Two Ways

The notion that there are two well-defined paths would have been familiar to a Jewish audience (#1b, #1h). Psalm 1, for instance, contrasts "the way of the righteous" with "the way of the wicked." The first-named are defined as those who "delight . . . in the law [Torah] of the Lord" (Ps 1:2). Standing in this tradition, it is no surprise that the Jesus movement was known in some circles as "the Way" (Acts 9:2; 19:9, 23; 22:4; 24:14, 22). This was undoubtedly due to the fact that its members were trained in "the way of salvation" (Acts 16:17), "the way of the Lord" (Acts 18:25), or "the way of God" (Acts 18:26)—terms used repeatedly in the Septuagint. In 2 Peter false teachers are spoken of as having left "the way of truth" (2:2), "the right way" (2:15), "the way of righteousness" (2:21) in order to follow "the way of Balaam" (2:15). According to the Q Gospel, Jesus contrasts "the narrow gate" with "the wide gate" (Matt 7:13-14; Luke 13:23-24). The former "way is hard" but "leads to life" while the latter "way is easy" but "leads to destruction." In each of these cases the two-way mentality is evident, yet, in none of them is there the suggestion that the *Didache* was known or used to flesh out the exact meaning of the Way of Life.

Within the Hebrew Scriptures, Jeremiah was sent by the Lord to say to the people: "Behold I set before you the way of life and the way of death" (Jer 21:8). In the *Apocalypse of Baruch* (c. 100 C.E.) the Jewish author writes that the Lord "established a covenant for them at that time and said, 'Behold I have set before you life and death'" (19:1). Similar passages can be found in Deut 11:26-28; Prov 2:1-22, 4:18-19; *Sib. Or.* 8:399. All in all, the Way of Life and the Way of Death served as evocative metaphors for giving voice to the challenge the Lord God made to Israel.

The Way of Life Defined by the Negative Golden Rule

The *Didache* defines the Way of Life using two functional definitions. The first definition summarizes positively what must be done; the second definition summarizes negatively what must be avoided. The first definition summarizes one's relationship with God, the second with one's neighbor.

The Way of Life was frequently characterized as loving God. Twice each day, in the morning and the evening, for example, Jews recited the *Shema* (Bradshaw 1992:19). The first line begins, "Hear, O Israel: The Lord is our God," and the second continues, "You shall love the Lord your God . . ." (Deut 6:4-5). In Mark's Gospel, accordingly, when a scribe asks Jesus what is the "greatest commandment," Jesus responds by reciting these very same lines (Mark 12:29-34) and the scribe commends him for so doing. In Luke's Gospel, the scribe is described as "a lawyer" who asks not for the "greatest commandment" but, "What must I do *to inherit* eternal life?" (Luke 10:25). Jesus turns the question back to his inquirer, "What is written in the law [Torah]? How do you read?" (10:26). In this portrait the inquirer delivers the second line of the *Shema* and the positive Golden Rule, and Jesus commends him, saying, "You have answered right; do this and you will live" (10:28). Thus, whether on the lips of Jesus or on the lips of a Jewish lawyer, the *Shema* served to specify the "greatest commandment" and the route to "eternal life." This naturally shows up in the *Didache* as the first functional definition of the Way of Life.

The joining of loving God and loving neighbor would also be foundational within Judaism. According to the *Mishnah* the priests in the Temple recited the decalogue prior to the *Shema* (*m. Tam.* 5:1). In the first century *Testaments of the Twelve Patriarchs*, Dan teaches his sons, "Love the Lord throughout your life and one another with a true heart" (*T. Dan* 5:3), and Issachar tells his, "Love the Lord and your neighbor" (*T. Iss.* 5:2). Philo (d. 50 c.e.), when describing the special commandments given to the Jews by God, notes that everything can be divided into two categories: (1) "the regulating of one's conduct toward God by the rules of piety and holiness" and (2) "[the regulating of] one's conduct toward men [and women] by the rules of humanity and justice" (*Special Laws* 2.63).

The Way of Life as Implying an Apprenticeship

After defining the Way of Life using the dual definitions the *Didache* turns its attention to "the training [required for the assimilation] of these words" (1:3). As explained above, the definitions of the Way of Life and the Way of Death served to frame the main attraction, that is, "the training" program that occupied 78% of Part I and 36% of the entire *Didache*. Since 36% of the entire *Didache* is devoted to this "training," it is not surprising that the entire manuscript was, at some point in time, given the title *didachē*.

The Greek word *didachē* makes reference to the training that a master-trainer *(didaskalos)* imparts to apprentices or disciples. In classical Greek, basket weaving, hunting with a bow, and pottery making represent typical skills transmitted under the term *didachē* (*TDNT* 3:135). For our purposes here it is significant to note that the verb *didaskein*—customarily translated as "to teach"—was normally used to refer to a prolonged apprenticeship under the direction of a master: "Thus, *didaskein* is the word used more especially for the imparting of practical or theoretical knowledge when there is a continued activity with a view to a gradual, systematic, and therefore all the more fundamental assimilation" (ibid.).

When one examines the particulars of the training outline it is apparent that one does not arrive at the skills necessary to "love those who hate you" (1:3c) or to "judge with justice" (4:3) merely by being told to do so on one or two occasions. Accordingly, while all the English translations prepared to date have been content to translate *didachē* as "teaching," it is evident that the force of *didachē* is better rendered as "training" or "apprenticing." Moreover, in our contemporary society "teaching" is associated with classroom instruction, and in the popular mind this often evokes the passing on of information from professor to student. The word "training," on the contrary, has the advantage of suggesting the dynamics of an apprenticeship wherein novices gradually and progressively assimilate the performance skills of a master-trainer *(didaskalos)*. In what follows, the terms "master-trainer," "mentor," and "spiritual parent" will accordingly be used in preference to "teacher" to identify the one who trains.

Whether Each Novice Had a Single Mentor

The *Didache* offers evidence suggesting that each novice was paired off with a single spiritual master. The principal clue for this is the fact that the entire training program (save for *Did.* 1:3) addresses a single novice using the second-person singular. If, under normal circumstances, a single spiritual master were assigned the training of many or all the novices within a community, one would have expected that the second-person plural would have been used throughout. Furthermore, within the Way of Life training program the novice is instructed to actively remember and mull over the life and the training of "the one speaking to you the word of God" (4:1). The use of the singular here points in the direction of each novice having a single master. So, too, when regulations are put forward for choosing the water for baptism (7:2-3) and for ordering "the one being baptized to fast beforehand" (7:4), in each case the singular is used, again confirming the expectation that each candidate was baptized individually by a single individual—presumably the one who was his or her spiritual mentor and parent.

The *Didache* does not tell us how someone attracted to the Way of Life would come to have a spiritual mistress or master. One can surmise that the one coming forward to request admission would do so because of a keen admiration felt for the Way of Life of one or more members. Since the community gatherings were closed to outsiders (9:5), this limited personal attraction would be the basis for seeking admittance (4:10). If the community member to whom the potential candidate was initially attracted did not have the time, the temperament, or the skill to train a novice, one can further imagine that the community would have discussed among themselves who would be best fitted by virtue of sex, age, availability, temperament, state of life, and spiritual advancement to serve as spiritual master in the case of a particular candidate coming forward.

Since women in the ancient world were accustomed to being trained by other women (#1g, #2b), and since it would have been a source of scandal for a man to be alone for prolonged periods with a woman unrelated to him, it would be presumed that, save for special circumstances, women were appointed to train female candidates and men were appointed to train male candidates.

Remembering One's Mentor, the Presence of the Lord, and "Trembling"

Those who trained novices were not transmitting something of their own creation. Rather, such masters were "speaking to you the word of God" (4:1), hence something they themselves had received. When one explores the eucharistic prayers it will become apparent that Jesus is identified as "the servant who revealed the Way of Life." The master, in consequence, was also understood as a servant of the Father revealing to the novice the Father's wisdom for living. Where his "dominion" was addressed and taking effect in the life of the novice, there and then the *Didache* speaks of the presence of the Lord being felt: "there the Lord is" (4:1).

The *Didache* notes, in passing, that the novice becomes one "trembling through all time at the words that you have heard" (3:8). Here again the internal clues of the *Didache* demonstrate that the Way of Life was not received as mere information. Having been set upon the path of life by "the God who made you" (1:2), the novice trembled with excited anticipation and reverential fear. This was the way Israel originally experienced the word of the Lord from Mount Sinai (Exod 19:16) and the way others after them came to discover the transforming power of God's word (e.g., Ezra 9:4, Isa 66:2, Hab 3:16). Thus among the rabbis it was a commonplace to remember that every master taught his disciples "with awe and fear, with trembling and trepidation"(*b. Ber.* 22a) (#1h).

Praying for Enemies and Turning the Other Cheek

In terms of an orderly progression of topics, however, the initial section dealing with praying for enemies and turning the other cheek would appear to be placed at the head of the training program because new recruits had to be immediately prepared to respond to abusive treatment by outsiders (1:3-4). When examined in detail (Milavec 1995), the "enemies" in this case were not highway robbers or Roman soldiers, but relatives and friends who had become "enemies" due to the candidate's new religious convictions. Thus praying and fasting (#4c) for such "enemies" provided the necessary orientation for sustaining a comprehensive nonviolent surrender to the abusive family situation hinted at in *Did.* 1:4.

Among other things it was envisioned that the abusive family situation would lead to the forcible seizure of the novice's goods (1:4[D]), and the candidate was instructed to yield completely to such hostile acts and, at the same time, to surrender his or her goods to beggars (1:5), not because of any compulsion, but simply because the "Father" wished it. Implicit here is the contrast between a natural father who may be authorizing the tight-fisted seizure of his daughter's or son's assets with that "new Father" who generously gives to all and invites imitation. It is not possible to understand the text as addressing such existential needs at the beginning of the training process unless it is presumed that the *Didache* reflects a training process fashioned and modified over a period of time to address the situation of real candidates.

The Two Rules of Giving

Within the training program the issue of giving is taken up at the very beginning and again near the very end. The first instruction on giving (1:4) is in the present imperative and represents the kind of giving the candidate was expected to practice immediately upon entering into his/her apprenticeship. The second section on giving (4:5-8), however, is much more than a reinforcement of the earlier giving. Now everything (save *Did.* 4:5) is presented in the future tense and the focus is on the routine "taking and giving" and the much more extensive "partnering" of all one's resources "with your brother [or sister]" (4:8) (#2m, #2o). The future tense used here could function as a mild imperative (as in English), but this would leave an awkward situation in which two diverse rules of giving are provided and no attempt is made to harmonize them. On the other hand, if one examines the second set of rules for giving one discovers that this later giving involves sharing one's resources with members of the community—a situation that would prevail only after the time the candidate had gained admittance as a full member of the movement through baptism. These two sections on giving, far from being a senseless repetition occasioned by the mindless combining of preexistent sources, represent a thoughtful progression wherein the giving of the first kind aptly develops habits of mind and practice that prepare for and ensure the kind of giving necessitated by baptism. Since the first rule of giving is intended for immediate implementation it is presented as an imperative. The second section on giving, being in the future tense, then accurately reflects preparing for what is to come and is not yet. Here, again, by allowing that the *Didache* is more than a wooden collage of sources and that it reflects a training program in action one can gain hints about the pastoral genius underlying its composition.

How the Jewish Decalogue Was Adapted for Gentiles

The negative Golden Rule concerns itself with avoiding "as many things as you might wish not to happen to you" (1:2). *Did.* 2:2-6 proceeds to spell these things out in detail. First a decalogue (#1m) adapted to gentiles is offered. Then five speech failings and five evil dispositions are prohibited. All of this is then brought to closure by naming three classes of persons (2:7): (a) those whom one is bound to lovingly reprove: misbehaving members (looking ahead to 4:3 and 15:3); (b) those whom one cannot reprove and can only pray for: outside "enemies" (1:3) and insiders who are "shunned" (15:3); and (c) those whom one loves unreservedly and who generally need no correction: "mentors" and "saints" (4:1-2).

The framers of the decalogue (2:2) retained the linguistic structure in which the Lord delivered his Torah to his people on Mount Sinai (Exod 20:1-17, Deut 5:6-21). Thus one finds here the tenfold repetition of *ou/ouk* followed by a verb in the second person singular future tense. The use of the future tense works well here insofar as it indicates what the Lord will expect of those intent on loving him.

Since the novice could not have known what the Lord wanted him/her to be and do before this moment, the decalogue would not have been presented to the novice as a rebuke. This harmonizes with Jewish practice in training proselytes: no gentile was blamed for not having been raised as a Jew (Novak 1983:110–15; 1989:38). On the other hand it can be presumed that the novice asked questions relative to the scope of each of the terms of the decalogue and reflected on his/her own life in contrast to the Way of Life. These periods of clarification and self-examination might have passed over into feelings of regret or repentance.

In cases where this repentance spilled over into fits of depression or of self-negation the spiritual mentor must have been quick to remind the candidates that the Father in heaven was formerly unknown to them and that they were naturally misled by well-meaning parents and household gods. From this point on, however, the candidate would be expected to honor and to "love the God who made you" (1:2).

Why the Way of Life Omits the First Five Commandments

If the *Didache* deliberately omitted each of the first five commandments, what might this say about the social situation of novices preparing to enter the community?

1. The first commandment prohibits honoring any gods other than or alongside the one Lord. At the beginning of the *Didache* the Way of Life is defined as meaning "you will love the God who made you" (1:2)—thereby affirming, from the very start, a positive form of the first commandment. So, too, the *Didache* warns against becoming a diviner, an enchanter, or an astrologer (#1u), for these things lead to "idolatry" (3:4). After the close of the Two Ways the novice is told that eating "the food sacrificed to idols . . . is worship of dead gods" (6:3)(#3c). Hence one might conclude that the first commandment was omitted because it was redundant (#1n).

2. The second commandment prohibits making or using a "graven image" (Exod 20:4). For a gentile whose public buildings, private homes, and even the money used in the market place were routinely decorated with such images it would have been entirely unworkable to imagine that all of this could somehow be discarded, effaced, or replaced. Hence for gentiles the second commandment would have been nearly impossible to maintain unless they entirely abandoned their homes and cities. So one might conclude that the second commandment was omitted because not even God could demand the impossible.

3. The third commandment prohibits swearing a false oath while calling upon God to witness to the truth of what one is saying. The *Didache* has five speech infractions after its "decalogue." Swearing falsely is named first (2:3). Hence one might conclude that restating the third commandment at *Did.* 2:2 would have seemed redundant.

4. The fourth commandment prohibits profaning the seventh day with work. For gentiles the Sabbath rest (Exod 20:8-9) would have

imposed an unworkable expectation since the Roman lunar calendar governing public life made absolutely no provision for a cessation of work every seventh day (#4a). The "days of rest" named in the Roman calendar only occasionally coincided with the Jewish Sabbath, and even then such days were ordinarily devoted to public festivals in honor of this or that god. Since the members of the *Didache* community depended on the work of their hands, the fourth commandment would have imposed severe economic hardships. Hence one might conclude that the Sabbath rest was suppressed in order to safeguard a higher good (#1o).

5. The fifth commandment requires children to honor their parents. Gentiles could hardly be trained to honor their parents (Exod 20:12) when that "filial piety" so highly prized by Romans would have made the desertion of ancestral gods and the abandonment of their parental upbringing unthinkable (#12b) save in those instances when an entire patriarchal household converted to the Lord as a group (e.g., as in the case of the household of Cornelius in Acts 10). In the synoptic gospels one finds what John Dominic Crossan refers to as "an almost savage attack on family values" (Crossan 1994:58). Sayings such as "I have come to set a man against his father . . ." (Matt 10:35-36) and "Call no one your father on earth" (Matt 23:9) serve to illustrate how intergenerational strife (Crossan 1994:60) arose as parents endeavored to use their authority to block the conversion of their adult children. Given the implication of *Did.* 1:3-4 (namely that many or most novices were encountering hostile resistance to their conversion from parents and siblings), it became impossible for them to honor their parents and at the same time to honor the God of Israel. Accordingly, using a pattern of social displacement, novices preparing to enter the community are wisely directed to honor God as their true Father (1:5, 9:2-3, 10:2) and the members of the community as their true siblings (4:8). Thus again it appears that an obligation—in this case honoring parents—was suppressed in order to safeguard a higher good. Not even God could demand two contradictory commitments.

In retrospect the above discussion makes it evident that the omission of the second, fourth, and fifth commandments was not accidental. The framers of the *Didache* deliberately modified the Jewish decalogue in order to enable gentiles to walk in the Way of Life while continuing to live in Roman society. This in itself makes it clear that the Way of Life was not designed for use in the synagogue (#1j).

Why the Way of Life Adds Six New Commandments

If the deliberate omissions from the decalogue of Exodus 20 constituted pastoral adaptations, then one might suspect that the six additional prohibitions added to the *Didache's* decalogue were equally
purposeful. Properly speaking, the six break down into three pairs.

1. The first pair (A3 and A4) prohibits pedophilia and illicit sex
(porneia). A3 might be literally translated as "you will not corrupt boys"
(ou paidophthorēseis). Pedophilia was practically unknown among Jews
(*T. Levi* 17:11); hence it is not surprising that the Torah given to Moses
contains no mention of it. Outside of Judaism, however, pedophilia
was widely practiced and, within limits, was socially acceptable within
the Hellenized world (#1q). When the *Didache* specifically proscribes
sexually corrupting "boys" (2:2) it is singling out a practice that many
male neophytes had experienced firsthand as part of their early initiation. One should not imagine that the *Didache* was an innovator here,
however, since ancient Jewish authors amply demonstrated their re-
pugnance for this socially sanctioned pedophilia when writing to gentiles (#1q).

Along with pedophilia the decalogue introduces *ou porneuseis*—a
prohibition against *porneia* ("illicit sex"). The term *porneia* effectively
embraces "every kind of unlawful intercourse" (Bauer 693b). The commandments regarding "adultery" (#1p) and "pedophilia," consequently, appear to prohibit specific kinds of illicit sex. Why then does
the *Didache* insert a general prohibition against *porneia?* The original
ten commandments contained no such prohibition. However, entire
chapters of the Torah (Leviticus 18, 20) are devoted to spelling out a wide
range of prohibited sexual relations. Thus the framers of the *Didache*
must have added this commandment against *porneia* to signal to gentiles that the Way of Life required them to avoid such things as incest
(Lev 18:6-18, 20:9-12, 17, 19-21), intercourse with menstruating wives
(Lev 18:19, 20:18), and prostitution (Gen 38:24; Lev 21:9) (#1r).

2. The second pair of added commandments prohibits magic and
pharmakeuein, a term that literally meant "to give drugs" but could also
apply to the preparation of medicines while using incantations to
insure their supernatural efficacy (Kohlenberger 1065). The term
pharmakeuein can refer to "compounding poisons" (Niederwimmer
1998:89), yet in this context the term is linked not with murder but with
magic, as in the case of *Pseudo-Phocylides:* "Make no potions, keep away
from magical books" (149). Magic and potions did not compete with

the respectable religious rites of the established religions, but provided "the illegal insider dealing of people who were overambitious to achieve a personal end" (Fox 37).

3. The third pair of added commandments pertains to abortion and infanticide (#1s). These two prohibitions are closely linked and the addition of the post-partitive conjunction *de* ("and") signals this close connection. Since deliberate abortion and infanticide were not even considered as options in Jewish circles while, at the same time, they were widely regarded within Roman culture as a normal mode of family limitation (*ABD* 1:34; Fox 343), these two infractions were repeatedly underscored in the Jewish sources created for gentile instruction (*Pseudo-Phocylides* 184–85; Josephus, *Contr. Ap.* 2.202; *Sib. Or.* 2.281-85).

In sum, one can conclude that the framers of the *Didache* deliberately modified the Jewish decalogue to exclude precisely those injunctions that would have been impossible to maintain within a gentile cultural milieu and, on the other hand, to include three pairs of infractions that were particularly odious to Jewish sensibilities. Since all three pairs would have been condoned by most gentiles, the insertion of these pairs clearly implies that the novice was expected to alter his/her moral sensibilities during the time of his/her training. When it came time "to reprove against failings" (4:3) or to "confess your failings" (4:14), it can be surmised that the novice would be ready to judge and be judged by standards remarkably different from those prevailing in popular culture. The countercultural force of the *Didache* thus becomes apparent.

The Five Speech Infractions

After the decalogue five speech-infractions are proscribed, using the same linguistic structure found in the decalogue. The novice is first trained not to swear falsely *(ouk epiorkēseis)*. This clearly refers to the third commandment (Exod 20:7). Philo notes that this commandment requires that one tell the truth even when not invoking God as a witness (*Decalogue* 84). If one must swear an oath, however, Philo explains that this is tantamount to "calling on God to give his testimony concerning the matters which are in doubt" (*Decalogue* 86). Then the novice is warned against bearing false witness. This clearly refers to the eighth commandment: "You will not bear false witness against your neighbor" (Exod 20:16). Next, the novice is warned against speaking badly of anyone. The Torah specifically prohibits speaking badly of "father or mother" (Exod 21:16). The next injunction is against holding grudges (Zech 7:10, *Barn.* 2:8, *1 Clem.* 2:5). Finally, the novice is warned against being "double-minded or double-tongued" (2:4)—a reference to the person "who says one thing and thinks another" (Niederwimmer 1998:91). The final admonition is reinforced by an aphorism: "Being double-tongued is a snare of death" (2:4). The idea that an unruly tongue brings on death is widely attested in Jewish sources (Prov 13:14, 14:27, 21:6; Ps 17:6; Tob 14:10; Sir 28:13-26; *b. Arakh.* 15a-b). A positive mandate at the end enforces the requirement that, in every situation, what one says must find its completion in what one does.

Five Prohibited Dispositions

Following the decalogue and the five speech infractions, five injurious dispositions are proscribed (2:6). The first two dispositions (covetousness and greed) are associated: Both pertain to an inordinate attachment to goods. The last two dispositions (bad manners and arrogance) may also be associated, as both pertain to an inordinate attachment to one's own self-importance. These pairs frame the term "hypocrite," and one can imagine that the hypocrisy referred to is intimately linked with attachment to goods and to one's self-importance—a hint that needs to be applied when "hypocrites" (#4d) are encountered in fasting and praying (8:1-2).

Spiritual Parenting

The Greek expression *teknon mou* literally signifies "my offspring" without regard for age or sex. In this context it cannot be supposed that the master-trainer is the biological father or mother of the novice. Within the Septuagint *teknon mou* is already used metaphorically as an intimate form of address (Gen 43:29) or to denote a novice in relationship to a trainer and mentor (1 Sam 3:16; 26:17). The gender-inclusive term aptly captures the fact that the *Didache* addresses women and their concerns. In contrast, Jewish wisdom literature typically addresses the gendered "my son" and then proceeds to warn against such things as being intoxicated by loose women (e.g., Prov 5:20). Even the Sermon on the Mount, when closely analyzed, exclusively addresses men and male concerns.[5] The wisdom of the *Didache*, therefore, stands apart by deliberately offering training to women. Such training ensured that women were empowered to be active participants within community affairs[6] and "does not concern itself with rendering a household code whereby wives are subordinate to their husbands" (Rose-Gaier in Crossan 1998:371).

If one extrapolates the evidence even further one might imagine that the appearance of "my child" at the midpoint of the training program may signal the tragic case of many novices who, by this point, have despaired of winning over their biological fathers and/or mothers by prayer and fasting (1:3). In the face of this loss such persons would have the need to bear their grief and share their struggles with another "father" or "mother" who stands for them and with them in their new commitments (#1t).

---

[5] In Matthew 5–8 training is directed first and foremost to men. Phases like "angry with his brother" (5:22) and "your brother has something against you" (5:24) and "eye of your brother" (7:4) reflect the Mediterranean world in which men inhabited the public spaces and needed to make peace with each other. The women in the courtyards, meanwhile, are silently passed over. Jesus' observations about the one "looking at a woman lustfully" or "divorcing his wife" (5:28, 31) again capture only the male point of view.

In contrast, while the *Didache* focuses on issues that apply particularly to women (2:2[A8]; 13:5), other aspects apply particularly to men (2:2[A3]; 13:3). The household codes of *Did.* 4:9-11 are noticeably inclusive. In fact, my gender-inclusive translation makes it evident that women and women's issues were being addressed throughout the *Didache*. See n. 4 above.

[6] The only function specifically reserved for men was the one in which negotiations with outsiders (nearly always men) were mandatory (15:1). Niederwimmer interprets *Did.* 15:1-2 to mean "that the local officials, together with the prophets and teachers (or, to the extent that the last two groups are absent, they alone) lead the worship service that formerly was in the hands of the prophets and teachers alone" (1998:202; also held by Catholic scholars, such as Schillebeeckx 1981:23). Willy Rordorf, for his part, reads *Did.* 15:1-2 in a more radical manner: "the bishops and deacons are charged to replace them" as presiders at the Eucharist (1998:228; also held by Catholic scholars such as Raymond E. Brown 1980:336). Schöllgen, in contrast, takes the position that "these matters remain in the dark" (1996:59). Going beyond Schöllgen, I would argue that the *Didache* provides sufficient evidence to decide that neither the prophets nor the bishops presided at the Eucharist (see #6o and #9f). From my reading of the evidence the presider at the first Eucharist would have been the presider at the baptism, namely, the mentor who had "fathered" or "mothered" the candidate. Space prohibits me from developing this topic here. One can be sure, however, that if women were being trained by women, then the logic of the text and of the culture would lead us to surmise that these same women were baptizing those whom they had trained and presiding at their first Eucharist.

The Five Fences

Didache 3:1 serves as a fitting opening to the five illustrations of how to avoid major infractions by keeping guard against minor infractions that might not be serious in themselves but that form a slippery slope toward great infractions. In Jewish circles this would be recognized as erecting a "fence" (#1v). The linguistic repetition is evident in each of the five cases and, quite evidently, *Did.* 3:1-6 formed an oral unit bound together by a single logic.

The progression of the five topics, however, remains puzzling. In the Sermon on the Mount Jesus offers five illustrations of how the righteousness of his disciples must exceed "that of the scribes and Pharisees" (Matt 5:20), but only murder and adultery are treated in common with those topics named in the *Didache*. The flow of topics, meanwhile, does not parallel what one finds in the decalogue, save again for murder and adultery. Murder and adultery were the gravest sins against one's neighbor; hence it is no surprise to find them treated first by the framers of the *Didache*. Idolatry comes next. Hence one must suppose that the framers of the *Didache* were acutely aware that gentile converts had to be warned against seemingly innocent practices that formed the path leading to idolatry. The same holds true for thefts and blasphemies.

The first sequence warns against yielding to anger since "anger is the path leading to murder" (3:2). This seems evident enough and finds Jewish and Christian parallels (e.g., *T. Sim.* 2:6-7; 3:1-6; *b. Yoma* 75a; Matt 5:21-22). If one reads *zēlōtēs* as "envious," then a graded progression exists from envious to contentious to hotheaded to murderous. The implied message is clear: "Check the beginnings lest you proceed any further down this path." In the Gospel of Matthew, Jesus begins by warning against anger but then passes on to consider insults and name-calling, issues that find no parallel here.

The fifth sequence might appear as puzzling since it associates grumbling as "leading to blasphemy" (3:6). The Greek term *blasphēmia* derives from *blaptō* + *phēmē* ("to injure" + "speech") and so could be rendered as "slander." In the Septuagint, however, this term is almost entirely used to denote injurious speech against the Lord, hence what is commonly called "blasphemy." Since the verb *gonguzein* ("to murmur") is used repeatedly to describe the grumbling of the Israelite people in the desert (Exod 16:2, 7(2x), 8(2x), 9, 12), some scholars believe this is the implied case history that stands behind the warning against murmuring (Ross 218). While an individual mentor might have used this case history to illustrate the meaning of *Did.* 3:6, the text itself does not give any hint in this direction (Niederwimmer 1998:99).

In the wake of a list of positive virtues to be cultivated (3:7-9) it comes as no surprise that the novice was then trained to regard everything as happening providentially: "You will accept the experiences befalling you as good things, knowing that, apart from God, nothing happens" (3:10). In the face of sickness, poverty, failure, misunderstanding, therefore, the novice had to learn to reinterpret such "misfortunes" as "good things" ordained by God. Epictetus, a first-century Cynic philosopher, made this same point by calling his disciples to take an oath "never to distrust, nor accuse, nor murmur at any of the things appointed by God" (*Discourses* 1.14). In brief, Epictetus advised his disciples "to make the best of what is in our power and take the rest as it occurs" (*Discourses* 1.1). "And how does it occur?" Epictetus responded: "As God wills" (*Discourses* 1.1). Thus even many pagans would easily have grasped how murmuring or grumbling regarding one's lot could lead to blasphemy ("cursing God") (3:6).

The Art of Reconciliation

Being a realistic program, the *Didache* no sooner holds out the future promise of finding "rest" among the "saints" (4:2) than it turns to the darker side: "dissension" and "fighting" (4:3). The novice will be given an active role in preventing or defusing the harmful effects of such community-splitting conduct. The actual practice of reconciliation and judging is expanded in 15:3, but at this point the future tense signals what the novice has to anticipate after becoming a member of the community. When he or she is actually a member the details of this practice will be fully explained and illustrated.

Three Special Household Rules

After dealing with the sharing of resources the *Didache* puts forward three household rules. Taken together, the three rules imply that the typical candidate had children and slaves (#1x). The owning of slaves was not something reserved for the very rich since craftspeople

(#2a) of ordinary means frequently purchased one or more slaves to work with them in the family business.

In the case of children, they were to be trained from their earliest years "in the fear *(phobos)* of God" (4:9). The *Didache* does not give any guidelines as to when and how such children were to be introduced into the community. No provisions, for example, are made for infant baptisms (#3g). Nor, for that matter, did the framers of the *Didache* imagine that parents trained their children "in the Way of Life." Presumably, since the choice for the community was an adult decision prompted by the Spirit (4:10b), parents were expected to train their underage children in appropriate ways until such time as they came forward, in early adulthood, and asked for admittance. In any case, parents were not to withdraw their guiding and protecting hand from their children.

In the case of slaves the issues were more complex. Within pagan households it was taken for granted that household slaves served the same deities to whom their masters were attached. In a Christian household, however, this was not to be the case. The overall sense of *Did.* 4:10 appears to be that God calls masters and slaves alike without regard to their social status; hence masters must not despise their slaves or treat them harshly, for they are clearly "the ones hoping in the same God as you" (4:10a). Then the spiritual mentor addressed the slaves directly. This might be a hint that the training took place in the home of the candidate, where household slaves were naturally present. The central point appears to be that slaves, hearing that their masters have limitations, ought not to take this as an excuse to lose respect or take advantage of them. Just as in the case of children, slaves were expected to "fear the God who is over both of you" (4:10) until such time as they were moved, under the impulse of the Spirit, to ask to be initiated into the Way of Life. Thus the mentor (and not the master or mistress) admonished the household slaves then present to be subject to their "lords" (masters) and to obey them as representatives of God with the same "shame and fear" (4:11).

The Solemn Final Admonitions

Immediately after *Did.* 4:11 the novice is told to "hate every hypocrisy and everything not pleasing to the Lord" (4:12). This generalized rule would appear to stand in for all the cases not considered during the time of training and to be a consequence of what went immediately before: the novice is bound to please his or her Lord just as household slaves were bound to please their masters.

The second admonition recalls that everything received must be "guarded" as "the rules of the Lord"—again emphasizing the source and character of the training received (recall *Did.* 4:1). Furthermore, *Did.* 4:13 appears to imply that what has been received and memorized is the totality of the training program, neither more nor less. This final admonition must also signal that some have endeavored to alter what has been set forth. This issue will come up again in *Did.* 11:1-2, and the prophets will be named as the expected troublemakers in this realm.

The final admonition points to the future: "in church [i.e., in the assembly], you will confess your failings" (4:14). The framers of the *Didache* thereby insured that the particulars of the Way of Life would be the weekly framework for an examination of conscience and public admission of failure. For the moment the candidate is unfamiliar with the Eucharist; hence the details of *Did.* 14:1-3 are not presented. This will come later. For the moment it suffices that the novice be forewarned that a regular confession will take place in the assembly and that this confession ensured that "you will not go to your prayer in an evil conscience" (4:14).

Warning Against Innovators

All in all, the opening chapters of the *Didache* are devoted to a training program calculated to pass on and preserve a way of life. Here one finds the repeated use of the imperative, systematic attention to details and, most especially, sober warnings against those who might water down, change, or undercut what has been put forward (4:13; 6:1; 11:2). Taken together, these traits signify that the framers of the *Didache* had a personal investment in preserving a training program that might not always have been consistently and completely operative in the preparation of new members for baptism.

Food Prohibitions

The absolute prohibition against eating "the food sacrificed to idols" (6:3) occurs after the conclusion of the training program and just prior to baptism. One could imagine that the sources used by the editor of the *Didache* placed this outside the Way of Life instruction and, as a result, the editor was constrained to make an awkward addition after the close of the Two Ways section. On the other hand, the placement of this important and absolute injunction may have evolved in order to address a practical purpose. As long as candidates were in training they were obliged to refrain from attending the sacred community meals (9:5). Of necessity, therefore, most candidates would have been constrained to take part in family meals wherein, either regularly or periodically, some offering was made to the household gods as part of the meal or some portion of the meats served had been previously offered at a public altar. Only when baptism was just a few days away, therefore, could the candidate be expected to be bound by this new rule.

The Rite of Baptism

Once the *Didache* declares its preference for flowing water, it immediately provides exceptions for occasions when flowing water is not available (7:2-3). The "other water" allowed in exceptional circumstances is still or standing water (Rordorf 1972:506; Barnard 139 n. 3). Nothing is said regarding any emergency on the part of the person being baptized; hence, following the logic of the text itself, the *Didache* must be read as implying that some places did not have the preferred water and thus alternatives were being set forth. In the case of still water, however, cold water was to be given preference over warm, undoubtedly because it was closer to natural, flowing water (#3i). If neither cold nor warm standing water was available in sufficient quantity, then the one baptizing might, as a last resort, douse the person by pouring water over the head three times.

The *Didache*, using the aorist imperative, instructs those baptizing: "Immerse in the name of the Father and of the Son and of the Holy Spirit" (7:1). It would be misleading to imagine that one has here a "baptismal formula" (as suggested by Kavanagh 38, Rordorf 1972: 504–505, Niederwimmer 1998:126) and that baptisms were performed, as today, with the minister saying, "I baptize you in the name of the Father, etc." Had such a formula been used, one would have expected the entire formula to be spelled out, as is the case with the eucharistic prayers. Furthermore, the Hebraic expression of acting "in the name of X" has to do with the way a disciple or a servant is authorized *to act*, because of the training or mandate received from the master. According to the Christian Scriptures, for example, the Twelve heralded the reign of God and apprenticed disciples "in the name of Jesus" (Acts 4:18; 5:28; 9:27, 29). At other times they are presented as baptizing (Matt 28:19; Acts 2:38; 8:16; 10:48; 19:5; 22:16), healing (Acts 3:6, 16; 4:7), and exorcising demons (Acts 19:13-16) in this same name. Contrary to a widespread misunderstanding, "there is in the New Testament no belief in magically [or even supernaturally] potent names; in fact, there are no mysteriously dreadful words or names at all" (*TDNT* 5: 278).

Once it becomes clear that the trinity of names did not constitute a liturgical formula, one has to ask whether the action of immersing constituted the entire rite. This seems improbable. In fact, the *Didache* specifically points to the words of the rite with "having said all these things beforehand" (7:1). Thus every baptism was an affirmation of the Way of Life and a warning against the Way of Death. Most probably the candidate and the one who trained him/her entered into the pool of water where the baptism would be performed. One can imagine that the assembled believers formed a circle around the two. The trainer would then be in a position to face the candidate and address him/her with the words of life. Thus what the *Didache* calls the "word of God" (4:1) would be addressed to the candidate in the second person singular by his or her spiritual father or mother. The candidate would already know how to find the presence of the Lord in these words because of his or her training.

The closing line, "This is the Way of Life!" (4:14b), probably served as a liturgical refrain and, quite possibly, following Jewish parallels, was sung (#5a). The mentor reciting the Way of Life might have chosen to inflect the ending of certain lines (e.g., the last line of 1:3, 4, 6; 2:2, etc.)—immediately signaling that the entire community should come in, chanting in unison, "This is the Way of Life!" Alternately, the mentor may have recited this line boldly at given points as a signal that all were to chant the refrain together. Thus at one and the same time the candidate would recapture the warm feelings associated with hearing the words of the Lord voiced by his or her spiritual parent and the chanted refrain would bring home that the spiritual "family" found their identity within this same Way of Life. Then, once the Way of Life was finished, the Way of Death would be defined and repudiated. Here again the line "may you be saved, o children, from all of these things" (5:2b) probably served as the liturgical refrain and repeatedly emphasized the ultimate blessing offered by the community (see 16:2).

All in all, the rite of baptism most probably took place according to the following schema (see flowchart in appendix):

1. Community gathers in the place of baptism (most have been fasting for two days).

2. Candidates are led in by their spiritual mentors (all grow silent).

3. Mentors recite the Way of Life and Way of Death with the appropriate refrains.

4. Each candidate is immersed, dried off, and reclothed in a dry tunic.

5. New members are warmly embraced and kissed (same sex only) by their new family.

6. Lord's Prayer is prayed together for the first time.

7. All retire to a home for a fast-breaking feast (the Eucharist).

The Prebaptismal Fasting

Baptism marked a turning point. Social bonds were being broken and new ones were being forged. After baptism, every day would be spent visiting the saints and "rest[ing] upon their words" (4:2). Before baptism, however, most candidates probably felt the keen anticipation of entering into their new way of life along with the anxiety attendant upon the irreversible step that would cut them off from most of their family and friends. Anticipation and anxiety dulled the desire to eat (#3f). During these few days it is no accident that the candidate was told to fast (7:4). The one baptizing, along with able members of the community, fasted in solidarity with the candidate (7:4). During this period all "food sacrificed to idols" eaten by the candidates was expelled, and they were prepared for eating only pure and sacred food at the homes of "brothers and sisters," since the former communion meals binding them to ancestral gods would now be forever forbidden to them. The fast, therefore, hardly needed a theology. It was an experience looking forward to a promised future: more immediately inclusion within the community of saints, but later and more importantly inclusion in the final gathering from the four winds into the kingdom that the Lord God would establish when he came (10:5; 16:6-7).

The Lord's Prayer

As to prayer, the framers of the *Didache* took great pains to offer an alternative prayer to that used by "the hypocrites" (#4d). Three times a day the prayer "the Lord commanded" (8:2) was to be recited (#4g, #4h). The use of the plural in both the instruction and the prayer itself probably indicates that a group recitation was implied. This would not necessarily mean that the entire community would gather three times each day; rather, those working in the same shop or those in the same household would gather and pray. The framers of the *Didache* found no necessity to define the times during the day when these prayers took place. The silence of the *Didache* on this point suggests that everyone was familiar with those times because of the practice of the community, which in turn was shaped by the practice of the synagogue (#4f). According to Bradshaw, "the times were traditional and unchanged, and so need no explicit mention" (1982:26).

The *Didache* declares that members should pray "as the Lord commanded" (8:2). The "Lord," in this case, is not Jesus, for he is regarded as "the servant" who reveals "the life and understanding" of the Father (9:3). For early Christians, Jesus proclaimed "the good news of God" (Mark 1:14; Rom 1:1; 15:16; 2 Cor 2:7; 1 Thess 2:2, 9; 1 Pet 4:17)—never the good news of Jesus. Thus in each of the four places in the *Didache* where "good news" *(euangelion)* is found (8:2; 11:3; 15:3, 4) there is nothing to suggest that "Lord" refers to anyone but the Father (#10n). The "good news," therefore, is not a book or a gospel, but a message (Kelber: 144–47) (#11e). The Lord's Prayer, consequently, is the prayer of the Lord God delivered through his servant Jesus (9:3; 10:2). Furthermore, the prayer itself specifies what God is ready to do for those who trust in him, but only God could be counted on to know and reveal what God is getting ready to do (#10m, #10r). Thus the Lord's Prayer was not viewed as enumerating the expectations of Jesus but as revealing the promise of God to God's people.

The fourth petition is especially problematic and is commonly translated as "Give us today our daily bread." The fifth and sixth petitions deal with forgiveness (#3n) and temptations—seemingly the everyday stuff of life. Thus while most scholars are willing to find a future-looking expectation in the first three petitions, they regard the last three petitions as shifting over to "daily needs" (e.g., Gundry 1994: 104–10). Linguistically, however, the request for bread is expressed in the aorist imperative, which anticipates a single future action (as in the case of the first three petitions). In this light Raymond E. Brown pointed out that the Christian Scriptures supply instances where "bread" and "eating" are clearly equated with the future banquet in the Kingdom (Luke 6:21; 14:15; 22:29-30; Matt 8:11; Rev 7:16) (#4j). "This eschatological understanding of the petition for bread was the dominant one in the first centuries" (Jeremias 1971:200). The same logic holds true for the petitioned forgiveness. Again the use of the aorist imperative suggests a single future action. Moreover, placing "our debt" in the singular suggests that the total weight of the community's offenses will somehow come to light in the one-time final judgment. Only with difficulty can this be interpreted to mean that God is being petitioned to forgive individual sins daily. Finally, the "trial" (singular) to be overcome cannot refer to the daily "trials" or "temptations" encountered by individuals; rather, it points toward the common tribulation to be experienced by the righteous during the last days. In Raymond E. Brown's judgment: "The sixth and final petition is certainly eschatological . . . and the fifth is very likely eschatological. A noneschatological interpretation would leave the fourth [petition] isolated among the other petitions. But, in our opinion, a good case can be made for interpreting this petition eschatologically" (Brown 1961:195).

Linguistically, therefore, just as calling for the sanctification of the name and the arrival of the Kingdom are one-time events, so, too, the asking for the loaf using the aorist imperative presupposes it will be given only once (ibid. 197; see the caution of Meier 1994:362 n. 38). Since all six petitions of the Lord's Prayer are framed in the aorist imperative, therefore, it must be surmised that a one-time fulfillment is anticipated throughout. The Kingdom will come once. The loaf will be given once. Our debt will be forgiven once. We will be preserved from failing "in the trial" once.

Improvisation in Daily Prayers

While the rabbis tried to introduce some standardization into the prayer life of those who followed their lead, Jakob Petuchowski notes that "spontaneous expression of our deepest concerns" was always encouraged, following the mandate of Rabbi Eliezer: "He who makes his prayers a fixed task—his prayers are not [valid] supplications" (*m. Ber.* 4:4) (Petuchowski 1972:3, 9; Neusner 1988a:86; Sanders 1990:72). By "fixed task" the Babylonian Talmud understood either prayers offered "as a burden" or said by rote "in which one cannot say something new" (*b. Ber.* 29b). In fact, as late as the fourteenth century a Jewish liturgist wrote, "You will not find a single place in the world where the Eighteen Benedictions [the daily prayer] are word for word identical with the way in which the Eighteen Benedictions are recited anywhere else" (cited in Petuchowski 1972:9). Within the early Church one finds parallel expressions demonstrating that spontaneity was the normal expectation even when an abstract or schema was set out for guiding the prayer leader (#4n).

Within this milieu the Lord's Prayer can best be understood as forming an "abstract" of the six key themes that invited expansion by gifted prayer leaders and may also have served as a "synopsis" for those who lacked the gift of being able to improvise. Given the group orientation of the Lord's Prayer just considered, it would be hard to imagine that members of the Didache community assembled together to recite or hear recited a prayer that lasted a brief twenty seconds. Rather one can expect that in the presence of a gifted prayer leader the Lord's Prayer served to indicate the progression of themes that were expanded upon and added to in accordance with the specific circumstances and perceived needs of those present. Prayer books were not in use before the early medieval period; accordingly the oral giftedness of the prayer leader was always operative, interweaving familiar patterns of prayer with fluid expansions spontaneously arrived at. To this "enriched" version of the Lord's Prayer those present undoubtedly responded by reciting after the prayer leader the refrain, "Because yours is the power and the glory forever" (8:2). Everything noted here applies, with even greater force, to the eucharistic prayers (#5d). In fact, an examination of the structure of the eucharistic prayers suggests the possibility that the refrain was introduced by the prayer leader to close each of the six petitions of the Lord's Prayer.

The Eucharist

It is difficult to know precisely how the newly baptized responded to their first eucharist (#5j, #5o, #5q). Many, in the process of embracing the Way of Life, created enemies among those who regarded them as shamelessly abandoning all piety—piety to the gods, to their parents, to their ancestral "way of life." Having lost fathers and mothers, brothers and sisters, houses and workshops, the newly baptized were now embraced by a new family that restored all these abundantly. The act of eating together with their new family for the first time (see 9:5) must thus have made a deep impression upon them. Now, at last, they could openly acknowledge their true "father" among the fathers present or their true "mother" among the mothers present. It must have been as though their whole lives were pointed in this direction: that of finding brothers and sisters with whom they would share everything—without jealousy, without competition, with gentleness and truth. The act of eating together foreshadowed the rest of their lives, for here were the faces of their true family sharing, in the name of the Father of all (the unseen host), the wine and bread that were the foretaste of their unending future together.

Undoubtedly the spiritual father or mother who presided at the consecration of cup and loaf (#5t, #9d, #9f) knew the candidate through and through and adapted the prayers to the understanding of the novice he or she had trained (#5c, #5d). The consecrated cup evoked the holy vine of David, the consecrated broken loaf evoked the life and knowledge of the Father (#5b). The former indicates that the Father had elected Israel and established a kingdom of promise through David, his servant (9:2) (#5e). The gentiles did not formerly know what marvelous things the Father did for David and his contemporaries. Jesus revealed them. Drinking the cup of the holy vine, therefore, allowed the newly baptized gentiles to solemnly affirm their divine calling and to join in fellowship with Israel and share its eschatological expectations. Yet the promises were not enough. The Lord required fidelity to the Way of Life he revealed to the Israelites through Moses. In the case of the gentiles, however, they received the bread of God's Torah—the Way of Life and knowledge of the Father—through Jesus, his servant. The newly baptized undoubtedly felt a great sense of gratitude for Jesus and for their "father" or "mother" who, being God's chosen servants, had personally revealed these things to them and who, during the Eucharist, had extended to them the cup of election and the bread of life.

Above all, the Eucharist of the *Didache* was profoundly forward-looking (#5r): Those whose lives were nourished on the broken loaf were earmarked for the final ingathering—for just as the grains forming the loaf were once "scattered over the hills" (9:4) and only later were kneaded and baked into one loaf, so those who ate the fragments of this loaf were also assured that the Father (#4i) would one day harvest them "from the ends of the earth" so as to gather them into his

Kingdom. Those who ate, therefore, tasted the future and collective promise the "one loaf" signified.

Then, with the dishes and the tables taken away, the prayers after the meal began. Now the newly baptized encountered the "holy name" of the "holy Father" that was "tabernacle[d] in our hearts" (10:2). Next, themes of creation and redemption were recounted (10:3). Then the Lord was called upon to remember his church (the assembly), "to save her from every evil, to perfect her in your love, to gather her together from the four winds, sanctified, into your kingdom . . ." (10:5). Here the sentiments of the newly baptized might have found their most forceful stirring. "This new family to which you led me, this wonderful family I always dreamed of, may my Father who created all things save her . . . protect her . . . gather her."

Just as the message of the *Didache* continued the message of Jesus of Nazareth, so the Eucharist of the *Didache* perpetuated the proleptic foretaste of the Kingdom that marked the table fellowship of Jesus. Fed on the Eucharist, therefore, those who shared the Way of Life of the Father were nourished in their altered social reality. They were not of this world. Each day of the week they thought and acted in anticipation of the world to come (#10k). As brothers and sisters bound together under the direction of the same Father they shared their resources, their Way of Life, and their dreams. Each new Eucharist, consequently, celebrated the group identity, the standards of excellence, and the habits of judgment the community needed to champion in the name of the Lord. These early Christians, it must be remembered, faced a world that in so many ways had betrayed their trust and shattered their hopes. Thus with their eyes on the future they altered long-standing social barriers between Jew and gentile (#1o), male and female (#1f, #1g), slave and free (#1x). In their personal commitment to the future of God they fully expected that the Lord would honor their trust and fulfill their dreams. Clinging to each other, they clung to the promises of God, and in Jewish fashion (Vööbus 1968:164–68) they prayed: "Remember, Lord, your church . . ." (10:6) (#5h).

Prophets Praying at the Eucharist

The *Didache* was created for a community in which prophets were not vague memories from a past era but persons to be honored and reckoned with in its midst. Needless to say, such prophets were not the designated leaders of the community and, as a consequence, had no essential role in the training of candidates, in baptism, in Eucharist, in the correction of backsliders. The first mention of prophets in the *Didache* has to do with their honored role during the Eucharist, where they were permitted "to eucharistize as much as they wish" (10:7)(#6b). The Greek phrase *hosa thelousin* ("as much as they wish") could also be construed to mean "as often as they wish." Thus, given the nature of prophetic inspiration, this leaves open the possibility that this or that prophet would remain silent precisely because he or she was, at that moment, uninspired. A prayer leader was expected to function and, unless caught by a fever or struck by laryngitis, he or she would function according to skills at his or her command. The prophet, however, was understood to rely on an inspiration from the Spirit that blows when and where she wills (#6c). When the Spirit was active each inspired prophet gave thanks "as much as" he or she wished—a hint that when the prophets got rolling their combined ecstatic prayers might well run on over an hour. Lest this be considered preposterous, consider the case of the second-century *Martyrium Polycarpi*, where one discovers that Polycarp "stood up and prayed, being so full of the grace of God, that for two hours he could not hold his peace" (7). Yet for those present such charismatic prayers might have been expected to so grip their souls that time stood still and an hour passed quickly. The prayers and gestures of the eucharistic celebrant might have been engaging, true, profound—provoking deep longings and offering fervent hope. The prophets, on the other hand, began with the closing eucharistic petitions of saving, perfecting, and gathering of the church (10:5) and transformed these into living and breathing expectations that those present were able "to taste and see"—provoking tears and trembling and jubilation. The prophetic eucharistizing, therefore, was the sweet dessert that culminated every eucharistic meal.

While the *Didache* offers no themes or outline that guided prophetic eucharistizing, it should not be imagined that the prophets gave thanks for anything and everything under the sun. The prophetic voice, it must be remembered, was uttered in the context of well-known and well-established eucharistic themes. In fact, while prophetic prayers might have inserted themselves during the natural breaks in the community's Eucharist (e.g., after *Did.* 9:2, 3, 4, etc.), the placement of *Did.* 10:7 would seem to suggest that the prayers of the celebrant came to an end before the community turned toward the prophets, relying on them to bring the eucharistic prayer of the community to a dramatic close. Assuming this to be the case, special attention must be given to the four disjointed eucharistic acclamations in *Did.* 10:6, which possibly represent the spontaneous shouts or chants of various members of the congregation who were caught up by the future expectation with which the prayer leader closed the official prayer (10:5). In light of *Did.* 10:7 that follows, it can now be suggested that these jubilant anticipations might have functioned in various ways: (a) in order to prime the prophets for their charismatic prayers of thanksgiving, (b) in order to summarize typical refrains that punctuated the prayers of the inspired prophets, and/or (c) in order to indicate the spontaneous shouts/ chants whereby the congregation affirmed the prayers of the prophets (#6n).

If wandering prophets were largely drawn from the ranks of those who had been dispossessed of their homes, their livelihoods, and their families due to the crushing economic system of Roman commercialization, as Crossan suggests (1998:330–44) (#6h), then it could be surmised that the prophets had been broken in spirit and, perhaps, in body as well by an enormous amount of personal suffering. The prophets felt that God and God alone was their sure advocate and expected liberator (Pss 10:1-18; 34:16-22; 37:7-13; 70:5; Isa 41:17-20; Job 5:8-16; 29:11-17). And because they relied upon God so completely, they prayed for the coming of the Kingdom with a fierceness and a rage that defied human understanding.[7] As they prayed, these apostle-prophets undoubtedly remembered the years of distress when, crop after crop, they slipped deeper and deeper into debt despite the backbreaking work of their entire family. Defaulting on their loans, they forfeited house and land and, as a result, a merciful lender might have allowed them to remain as tenant farmers on their own land—but now one-fourth to one-third of each crop had to be set aside as land-rent. But if a farmer was unable

---

[7] The rabbinic tradition provides a parallel case of how deep suffering nurtures urgent prayer. According to the *Mishnah,* when the seasonal rains fail to arrive at the expected time the people gather around the ark, which has been brought forward "in the street of the town," and "they bring down before the ark an experienced elder who has children and whose cupboard is empty" (*m. Taan.* 2:2). Note that the prayer leader must be someone *respected*, someone *skilled* in improvising the daily prayers, and someone *suffering* at the cries of his own children for bread. This last qualification was very significant. The text explains why: "So that his heart should be wholly in the prayer" (2:2). The charismatic prayer of the prophets, then, must have derived from their enormous suffering, which gave birth to their enormous hope in the Lord.

to feed his family and pay the Roman taxes on his own land, how much more was he handicapped by land-rents and new loans for seed. Inevitably the farmer would be forced to sell his children into slavery—an act of mercy—for he could no longer provide food or clothing for them. Finally he would sell his beloved wife or send her back to her father's house. Then, bereft of honor and resources, he would flee his moneylenders and take on the life of a fugitive rather than be sold by his creditors into debt-slavery himself. For some men and women recently driven into such desperation, the prospect of the Kingdom of God opened up their last hope in this world. In fact, as prophets of this future they were able to regain a new identity and honor that wiped away their shame.

Danger Posed by Prophets

From this point onward almost all one hears about prophets is cautionary. The impression given is that the community had more to fear from abusive and wayward prophets than to receive from true ones. Lifestyle and charisma could just as easily tear down as build up "all these things said beforehand" (11:1). As Gerd Theissen has so artfully suggested, the prophets moved about with "no bread, no bag, no money in their belts" (Mark 6:8 and par.) (#6a). In response, the Didache communities agreed that the prophet-apostles ought to be "received as the Lord" (11:4) only as long as they adhered to their own self-definition as "passing through" (11:5) and "having no money" (11:6).

Even before the passionate anticipation of the Kingdom was heard in the prophet's prayer, members of the community must have felt it in their very style of living. Unlike the householders of the community who cherished their homes, their livelihood, their families, the prophets had seemingly been purified by suffering and let go of these things in order to devote every day to announcing, praying for, and anticipating the Kingdom of God. They blissfully counted on God to take care of them even when they did not know, from day to day, where their next meal was coming from. The life of the prophet, therefore, must have made a deep impression on the community even before their words were heard.

When they prayed or spoke in Spirit (#6q), the prophets' evident charisma would not be "put on trial or judge[d]" (11:7, 11). They would, however, be expected to have the "habits of the Lord" (11:8) (#6j) that were defined and understood by the community in its Way of Life. A prophet could "in Spirit" convene a eucharistic assembly (11:9) but could not presume to preside and supplant the established patterns for community Eucharist. Even when prophets might be present at the weekly Eucharist their evocative and spontaneous prayers were to be honored, but only to the degree that they added to and did not displace the community's control of its own rite. When it came to the way of the Lord, the prophets could freely act out the radical demands of their calling and feverishly anticipate God's future, yet they could not train others "to do as much" (11:11). The spirituality of everyday holiness was thereby secured against the excesses of apocalyptic fervor.

It is difficult to know what the *Didache* had in mind when it spoke of prophets "acting for the worldly mystery of the church" (*poiōn eis mystērion kosmikon ekklēsias*) (11:11) (#6k). This obscure phrase finds no explanation within the *Didache* and no exact parallel in either the secular or religious literature; hence it is impossible to designate precisely what the phrase meant for the community of the *Didache*. One can surmise, however, that an entire range of evocative and/or disturbing prophetic gestures were anticipated that were not to be judged or imitated "for with God he has his judgment; for just so acted also the ancient prophets" (11:11). Note that the emphasis is expressly upon a prophet having been tested and found "true" (11:11). Such tested prophets were effectively granted great liberty as long as they did not presume to train others that God required them to act likewise.

What might this include? Maybe a prophet undertook degrading tasks normally reserved for slaves—like cleaning toilets or washing the feet of visitors or dressing the wounds of lepers—with the idea of demonstrating that, when the Lord arrives, even the most demeaning acts of service will be understood rightly as cloaked with dignity and love. Then again, maybe another prophet said that the Lord had trained him to despise money and thus he took up the practice of referring to money as "shit" and made a vow never to touch it again. Another prophet may have refused to eat anything one or two days prior to any Eucharist in the expectation that, perhaps at this Eucharist, the Lord might come. At still other times a prophet might even hold up his own prophetic calling as an imitation of Jesus' way of "acting for the worldly mystery of the church."

It is misleading to imagine that "the worldly mystery of the church" ought to be narrowly interpreted against the backdrop of Eph 5:32 as "an allusion to women who accompanied the wandering prophets and whose relations to them were not unequivocal" (Theissen 1992:41). Niederwimmer sees it as "a spiritual marriage" between a prophet and a "sister" that, being a celibate union, "corresponds to its heavenly model, namely, the union of the *Kyrios* ['Lord'] with his bride, the church" (1998:182; 1996:329, 331 n. 34; Campenhausen 73 n. 119; Harnack 121–22; Rordorf 1978a:187). But the use of Eph 5:32 at this point is unjustified. If the framers of the *Didache* had wanted to address the "spiritual marriages" of prophets, they would have said so.

The pastoral genius of the *Didache* is that it knew how to honor the heroic virtue and charismatic gifts of the prophets without imagining that perfection consisted in doing these things (11:11). The *Didache* celebrated the love of God and neighbor (1:2) in the seemingly insignificant deeds of ordinary life: in daily prayers (8:2), in sharing resources (4:8), in reconciling those fighting (4:3). Prolonged prayers, selling all one had in order to give it to the poor, and reconciling the whole world to Christ were left to others—the few and not the many. In sum, therefore, the *Didache* held on to "the life and knowledge" (9:3; 10:2) of the Father as expressed in the Way of Life by way of taming the unmitigated excesses of the wandering apostle-prophets.

First Fruits Offered to the Prophets

The Jewish tradition of setting aside first fruits (#7a) for the Lord does not appear to have been the practice of any first-century churches (#7f) except for those following the *Didache*. Undoubtedly many pagans who embraced Christianity had the practice of offering first fruits prior to their conversion, and after their conversion they wanted to know how they were to offer their first fruits to the true Lord. Christianity had no shrines or temples and, more importantly, no priests ready to receive these first fruits. Accordingly the *Didache* took a bold and innovative step when it designated "the prophets" as the honorary "priests" (13:3) to whom members of the Didache community were to bring their first fruits. Now there was not a place but a person to whom the faithful could be directed when it came time for them to express their gratitude to the Lord.

It appears that the category of first fruits has a Jewish foundation that has been artfully adapted for gentiles making their living as craftspeople and merchants. Even such small details as the phrase "make dough [sitia]" (Niederwimmer 1998:191 n. 17) link the categories within a specifically Jewish mentality wherein the baked bread set aside for the priests later came to be referred to as the "dough offering" (Hebrew *ḥallah*). The extension of the offering of first fruits when "opening a jar of wine or oil" (*Did.* 13:6) or when receiving an augmentation "of silver and of clothing and of every possession" (*Did.* 13:7) finds no counterpart in ancient Judaism and might serve to suggest that craftspeople and merchants had as much cause to thank God for their prosperity as did the farmer and the baker. The novice, it will be remembered, was trained to regard everything he or she possessed as the Father's "free gifts" (*Did.* 1:5) and to "accept the deeds befalling you as good things, knowing that, apart from God, nothing happens" (*Did.* 3:10). In light of this understanding, undoubtedly the first and best products of the kiln, the loom, and the forge were set aside for first fruits and given to the prophets so that they could give thanks to God.

The anti-temple[8] stance of the *Didache* (#10q, 14b) and the decided preference for the Spirit-led prayers of the prophets helps explain why the first fruits were to be given to "the prophets," who were regarded as the most fitting substitutes for the priests of the Temple. Where prophets were absent the first fruits were given "to beggars" (13:4) who were, in effect, in many ways near equivalents to the prophets. Yet could not an artisan or merchant do this for himself? Surely—but not as warmly and graciously as the one who was broken by suffering through the loss of home, of family, of occupation. Moveover, when the evidence is pushed, the pastoral genius of the *Didache* is revealed in the surprising honor and dignity the members of the community conferred

[8] The *Didache* exhibits a systematic attempt to displace and demote the Temple cult even apart from substituting the prophets for the priests when it came time to offer first fruits: (a) The prayer rhythms of the Didache communities give not the slightest hint that one should, following the practice of many Jews (Pss 28:2; 138:2; Dan 6:10; *m. Ber.* 24b), face the Temple during prayer or make timely pilgrimages to the Temple; (2) *Did.* 14:1-3 has the effect of substituting the Eucharist as the "pure sacrifice" that, according to Mal 1:11, takes place "in every place and time" and "among the gentiles"—thereby making the Temple sacrifices not only unnecessary but contrary to "the divinely instituted rule of the Lord" (14:1); and (3) *Did.* 16:3-8 has the effect of recasting the end-time expectations in such a way that Jerusalem and the Temple will have no role whatsoever in the coming of the Lord-God and the establishing of the Kingdom of God in the future (#10q).

upon lowly vagabonds and beggars who, in God's eyes, were being chosen to receive the first and best gifts of God's creation.

Having the prophets offer prayers of thanksgiving for the simple gifts of prosperity undoubtedly set off internal contradictions. Those bringing first fruits came with light and happy hearts to the prophets who, for the most part, had abandoned all expectation of joy in this world. Yet in the receipt of the simple joy of a mother bringing a loaf of warm bread just out of the oven (13:5) it might be expected that the barefoot children giggling and hiding behind her skirts transported the prophet back to a happier time. Undoubtedly, on such occasions, many a prophet found himself or herself spontaneously shedding tears of postponed grief. As their tears flowed, the bottomless grief in their hearts lightened. In the end, therefore, bringing the first fruits to the prophets was calculated to apply a potent medicine for healing their grief and reviving their hope of entering into the simple joys of modest prosperity. In effect, *life did not have to stop and remain breathless until the Kingdom arrived.* Hence by degrees the prophets who settled in the Didache community learned to laugh again, and some began to work again. They returned to work because they felt ashamed (having worked all their lives) that others had to work harder to maintain their well-being. But more than this, they returned to work because their love of life was returning. And as they worked and gained a degree of self-reliance again, their passion for the coming of God burned less feverishly. With time the Spirit no longer provoked them with the same overriding obsession they had known earlier when it came to praying after the Eucharist. As they healed, therefore, the prophetic urge gradually left them entirely.

Stepping back, one notices that the Didache community made ample provision for welcoming prophets but gave no attention whatsoever to creating them and sending them out. Furthermore, wandering prophets were welcome to settle down—an indication that some prophets liked what they saw and knew of the Didache community. But even with prophets settling in the community with regularity, the distribution of first fruits had to anticipate a case when a prophet would not be present and the first fruits would have to be given to their nearest equivalent, beggars. This is an unsettling clue. On the face of it the Didache community appears to attract, absorb, and in the end to dissolve the prophetic spirit itself. This topic deserves further research, for it provides potential clues for understanding how and why prophecy faded in the early churches.

Confession of Failings and Eucharistic Sacrifice

Scholars have been puzzled by 14:1-3, for it appears that this section should have been presented prior to the eucharistic prayers (9:1–10:6) (#8k). On the other hand, if the earlier chapters presented the first Eucharist following the baptism of new members, the confession of failings would have been deliberately omitted for sound pastoral reasons. Thus the confession of failings and the discipline of reconciliation are introduced in precisely the right place to prepare new members for their second and subsequent Eucharists.

When seen in context, the confession of failings in *Didache* 14 does not come as a complete surprise. At the very end of the catechumenate the novice was told, "You will not leave behind the rules of the Lord . . ." (4:13), and immediately thereafter he or she was given the means to sustain this attachment to the rules of the Lord: "[1] you will confess your failings, and [2] you will not go to your prayer with a bad conscience" (4:14). Two processes were named. Few particulars were given. Both were described in the future tense since both processes took place in the context of the Eucharist of which the novice had, as yet, no direct experience.

In 14:1-3 one finds a semantic parallel that elaborates 4:14. The positive activity of confessing has the positive effect of producing a pure sacrifice; the negation or absence of conflict has the effect of avoiding the negation of the pure sacrifice, namely, defilement. In both instances the motivation is clearly drawn in the direction of assuring the community that its sacrifice is "pure." The citation from the Lord nails down the requirement that a "pure sacrifice" (14:3) was an absolute requirement, for the Lord is a great king whose name must be "wondrous among the gentiles" (14:3c).

The Greek language distinguished between "sacrifice" *(thysia)* and "holocaust" *(enagismos)*. A "sacrifice" was "typically a festive daytime celebration with music and procession *(pompē)* toward the temple" (Jay 22). A "holocaust" was "commonly a nighttime ritual" (Jay 22) performed in silence (Jay:23), with the procession *(apopompē)* "leading away from the temple or city" (Jay 22). In both Roman and Greek circles a "sacrifice" had the effect of "joining people together in an alimentary [meal-sharing] community; it was life-enhancing and life-maintaining" (Malina 1996:33). On the other hand, the "holocaust" had the effect of "separating the person and group from defilement and danger; it was life-protecting" (Malina 1996:33). A "holocaust" was entirely burned on the altar and made no provision for a fellowship meal to follow. The sacrificial traditions of Israel also provided a clear demarcation between "sacrifice" (*zebach shelamim*, "sharing offerings," as in Leviticus 3) and "holocaust" (*olah*, "burnt offering," as in Leviticus 4) (Malina 1996:36).

The language of the *Didache* is entirely centered on "sacrifice" *(thysia)*; the term "holocaust" *(enagismos)* appears nowhere. This is entirely to be expected since "sacrifice" in the ancient world was commonly associated with a fellowship meal (#8c, #8i). Thus both Jews and gentiles would have been disposed to regard the eucharistic meal as a kind of "sacrifice" even though no animal was ritualistically killed. The absence of the term "holocaust" *(enagismos)*, meanwhile, signals that neither Jews nor gentiles would have regarded the confession of failings or the discipline of reconciliation as required for the forgiveness of sins or the atonement of guilt (#8b). Atonement, in the *Didache*, was associated with almsgiving (4:6), and divine forgiveness was principally an eschatological event (8:2; 16:2, 5).

Appointing Bishops Worthy of the Lord

Didache 15:1 instructs the congregation to "appoint . . . for yourselves" local overseers. Within the synagogues Jews were accustomed to elect "elders," and free elections also took place within various Roman associations and clubs (#9b). Since no superior authority (such as a founding apostle) exists to make local appointments, "the Didachist calls on the community to choose their own officers or representatives from among themselves" (Niederwimmer 1998:200). Three observations follow from the logic of the text itself:

1. The framers of the *Didache* present this rule without any fanfare or injunction of the Lord (as in *Did.* 14:3); hence one can presume that the communities had already been functioning according to this rule (Niederwimmer 1998:200). The rule should not be read as having any more solemnity than if the framers had said, "Keep up your good work at appointing worthy officers for yourselves."

2. The term *episkopos* ("bishop") (#9a) was, at this time, an entirely secular term for designating those "men" charged with oversight. The term carried no hint that those appointed were somehow to receive the office of teaching or presiding. The use of the term "bishops" therefore must be entirely divested of all later ecclesiastical associations if one is to properly understand it.

3. This rule for appointing overseers appears to be directed toward supporting the honor of these local overseers in the face of charismatic prophets and teachers (15:2). In effect, therefore, "bishops" were the underdogs who needed shoring up. More will be said regarding this shortly.

When speaking of bishops and deacons the *Didache* says they deserve honor because they exercise the *leitourgia* of the prophet-teachers (*Did.* 15:1). Niederwimmer interprets *Did.* 15:1-2 to mean "that the local officials, together with the prophets and teachers (or, to the extent that the last two groups are absent, they alone) lead the worship service that formerly was in the hands of the prophets and teachers alone" (1998: 202). Rordorf, for his part, reads the passage in a more radical manner: "the bishops and deacons are charged to replace them [the prophets]" (1998:228) as presiders at the Eucharist. Schöllgen, in contrast, takes the position that "these matters remain in the dark" (1996:59). I argue that the *Didache* provides sufficient evidence to decide that neither the prophets nor the bishops presided at the Eucharist.

In the Jewish synagogue structure "elders" were generally chosen from among the senior members of the most prosperous families within the community (Burtchaell 231; Draper 1995:292). As such they did not need community support. Elders gave themselves over to administration as a *leitourgia* and not as a remunerated service. In the Roman world this would be equivalent to the role of senator (*senator*), which was reserved for senior men of the notable families who filled the office out of a sense of civic duty (*leitougia*) and because it brought honor to their family name. Thus it is no mystery that both the verb and the noun show up in the *Didache*:

> *Leitourgeō . . .* means do[ing] public work at one's own expense. It is a political, almost legal, concept. The noun *[leitourgia]* means service for the people. In the later classical period it was as common as "taxes" today [as brought together in Rom 13:6] (Colin Brown 3:551; *TDNT* 4:217).

From this it becomes clear that *leitourgia* has to do with "unpaid public service" and not with "liturgy." Relative to bishops and deacons, therefore, the following points need to be taken into account: (a) the qualifications of the bishops and deacons give no hint of a liturgical function; (b) the ministry they undertook was an "unremunerated public service" (*leitourgia*) for which honor is due as in the case of the prophet-teachers;

(c) the "bishops" of the *Didache*, like their Jewish counterparts in the synagogue (Burtchaell 231; Draper 1995:292), were never understood as "priests" and never regarded as the "exclusive presiders" at the Eucharist (#9f); they would become so only as the result of developments during the second century.

Final Exhortation Regarding the End Times

The framers of the *Didache* provided its members with a synopsis of the last days (16:3-8). This synopsis is decidedly wary of the prophets and might have been framed to serve a number of purposes:

1. *God's Coming Is "Not Yet"*—First and foremost, *Didache* 16 served to challenge prophets tempted to cross the line between "coming soon" and "already arriving." Paul himself put forward a normative ordering of the events in the last days as the decisive scenario whereby the Thessalonians could safely dismiss false claims that "the day of the Lord is already here" (2 Thess 2:2) (#10b). The framers of the *Didache*, having encountered a similar problem, may have done the same. The stages leading to the end as defined in *Didache* 16 thus function as an existential safeguard against those who would claim that God is already on his way.

2. *Ordinary Holiness Is What Counts*—The introduction to the last days (16:1-2) clearly indicates that the framers of the *Didache* were not simply taking over readymade materials crafted by others. Preparing for the last days meant turning aside from all forms of heroic spirituality (e.g., prolonged fasting and praying, giving away or selling all one's possessions) in favor of "frequently gathering together" and "seeking the things pertaining to your souls" and remembering that "the whole time of your faith will not be of use to you if in the last time you should not have been perfected" (16:2). Thus, in the end, living the Way of Life is the common and most reliable road to perfection (6:2). Ordinary holiness is what counts. *Didache* 16 thus puts forward an existential safeguard against those who would claim that the last days call for radically new ways of being and of serving God.

3. *Beware of False Prophets*—The first century was plagued with a multiplicity of end-time scenarios. Many of these favored ways of thinking and acting that were antagonistic to the values of the *Didache*. By sanctioning a normative outline for eschatological expectations the framers of the *Didache* ensured that its own members were preserved

from what was of doubtful merit. At the same time the *Didache* fingered "false prophets and corruptors" (#10e) as the opening phase of the last days. Unlike nearly all other eschatological scenarios, therefore, the first menacing wave of evil emerges within the heart of the Jesus movement (#10g).

The internal havoc provoked by "false prophets" (16:3) opens the way to the second stage of the end-time scenario, namely, the appearance of "the world-deceiver" (16:4). While the *Didache* does not specifically say that "the world-deceiver" will set himself up in opposition to God, this is implied by the entire context. Thus according to the *Didache*, in the last days a final imposter (#10h) will massively succeed in being recognized as "son of God" due to "signs and wonders" (16:4b) making use of raw power. The use of "signs and wonders" to effect a general apostasy is a frequent theme in apocalyptic literature (#10i). As a result the inhabitants of the earth will "be betrayed into his hands" (16:4b)—again the focus is on the deceptive character of these "signs and wonders." Needless to say, a remnant faithful to the one true God (16:5) will refuse to accept "the world-deceiver."

One can only imagine what might be the "unlawful things that never have happened from the beginning of time" (16:4b). The Jewish imagination might be inclined to remember the so-called "desolating sacrilege" (Dan 11:31; 12:11; 1 Macc 1:54; 2 Macc 6:2; *Assumption of Moses* 8:5) consisting of statue of Olympian Zeus that Antiochus Ephiphanes set up in the Jerusalem Temple in 167 B.C.E. The Jewish imagination might also recall the persecution of the saints, as when Antiochus Ephiphanes had seven sons subjected to excruciating and prolonged tortures in the sight of their mother, who encouraged them throughout to remain faithful to the true God (2 Maccabees 7). These things were known to have happened. It is left to the imagination of the hearers, therefore, to conjure up yet worse things.

The Burning Process of Testing

The third phase of the apocalyptic scenario envisions all humans or/and their works as passing through "the burning-process of testing" (16:5a). The term *purōsis* ("burning-process") is a derivative of *pur* ("fire") and is only found once in the Christian Scriptures (1 Pet 4:12). *Dokimasia* has the sense of "testing," normally with the prospect of approving something, e.g., a team of oxen or a piece of gold (Bauer 202d).

This is precisely the construction one would expect if the "burning-process" functions both to approve and to destroy, as suggested by alternatives [a] and [b] that follow in the text.

The image of fire is frequently used in both the Hebrew and Christian Scriptures to evoke God's terrifying and mysterious presence (*TDNT* 6:936–37, 942–46). More especially, fire functions as the preferred metaphor for evoking the fearsome and consuming judgment of the Lord.

> In the prophets fire is one of the most common means of divine judgment. It smites both the vainglorious enemies of Israel (Amos 1:4, 7, 10, 12, 14; 2:2; Jer 43:12; Nah 3:13, etc.) and also the disobedient people of Israel itself (Amos 2:5; Hos 8:14; Jer 11:16; 17:27; 21:14; 22:7; Ezek 15:7; 16:41; 24:9, etc.). The close relation between images of judgment and theophany expresses the fact that fire is understood not as a blindly raging natural force but as an instrument of punishment in the hand of the divine Judge (*TDNT* 6:936).

Within the *Didache* the burning process has a dual function. The first is to entrap and to destroy those whom the Lord judges as unfit for the Kingdom. The Greek verb *skandalizein* comes from *skandalon* ("snare/trap") and literally means to cause someone to fall into a trap or snare (figuratively "into sin"). The literal sense works well here, for in the overall design of *Didache* 16 the framers of the *Didache* suggest that the world-deceiver had remarkable success in fooling many into imagining that he was "a son of God" (16:4a) and, by implication, to follow him in his ways. But the justice of God is not fooled; rather, it entraps and utterly destroys (*apollumi* being the emphatic form of *ollumi*) "the false prophets and the corruptors" (16:3a) along with "the world-deceiver" and his supporters.

The second function of "the burning-process" is saving those "having remained firm in their faith" (16:5b). One finds instances of this in the prophetic notion that God's judgment will destroy the wicked but purify the elect. Here the image of the refiner's fire is employed to suggest that the elect are like metals being purified as they pass through the final judgment (Isa 1:25-26; Jer 6:29; Ezek 22:20; 24:11; Zech 13:9; Sir 2:5; Prov 17:3). The prophet Malachi provides the clearest image of this dual functioning of the burning process when he explains that "the day of his [the Lord's] coming" will be like a "refiner's fire" (3:2). This fire "will purify the sons of Levi and refine them like gold and silver"

(3:2-3) while "the arrogant and all evildoers" among God's people shall be like straw in the oven: "the day that comes shall burn them up" (4:1). Texts within the Christian Scriptures that suggest this same dual function are rare and somewhat obscure (1 Cor 4:13-15; 1 Pet 1:5-9). Within the apocalyptic literature the destroying and tormenting dimensions of fire were more and more emphasized after the second century. In a few instances, however, the dual functioning of the burning-process was retained (e.g., *Apocalypse of Peter* 5–6, Lactantius, *Divine Institutes* 7:20-21). A succinct summary of this dual functioning is found in the Christian *Sibyllines* (second century):

> And then shall all pass through the burning river
> And unquenchable flame; and the righteous
> Shall all be saved, but the impious shall perish (2:252–54).

The closing words, "saved by the accursed it/him/herself" (16:5b), have been routinely interpreted as making a veiled reference to the crucified Christ. The Church Fathers (Harris 62–68; Taylor 100–101) and even the letters of Paul (Gal 3:3; 1 Cor 12:3) make reference to Jesus as "the accursed." Recent critical commentators such as Rordorf (1978: 198) and Niederwimmer (1989:265) accordingly conclude that "the accursed itself" evokes an appeal to the crucified Lord. This position, however, has three significant soft spots: (1) The internal logic of the *Didache* contains nothing that points in the direction of the soteriology of the cross; (2) when addressing issues respecting the confession of transgressions (4:14; 14:1) and the forgiveness of sins (4:6; 8:2), the framers of the *Didache* provide Jewish-inspired forms of logic entirely outside the context of the death of Jesus; (3) even the eucharistic prayers have their own internal logic and symbolism without in any way making use of any Pauline appeal to "covenant," "remembrance," or "the Lord's death" (1 Cor 11:25-26). In consequence, if the internal integrity of the *Didache* is to be allowed to stand, "saved by the accursed itself" (16:5b) ought not to be interpreted by a Pauline understanding foreign to the text itself.

The Signs of the Truth in the End Times

In the fourth phase three "signs of the truth" are specified. The Greek term *sēmeion* refers to "the sign or distinguishing mark by which something is known" (Bauer 747d). Such "signs" are very common within apocalyptic tracts (#10j) and ordinarily refer to momentous events that will occur just before the Lord's final coming. According to the *Didache* the world-deceiver appeared offering "signs" *(sēmeia)* (16:4b) that pulled the wool over the eyes of humankind. Now, with the likes of him destroyed, the time is ripe for new "signs" *(sēmeia)* to appear—"signs of truth" (16:6). Both of these events are linked with identical opening words: "And then will appear . . ." (16:4b, 6).

Didache 16:6 specifies three signs: (1) The unfurling [what?] in heaven; (2) the sound of the trumpet; and (3) the resurrection of the just (#15c). The first sign is the most difficult to comprehend. Harris was one of the first to note that the Greek text itself was ambivalent:

> The word *ekpetasis* is in its first idea [a] the spreading abroad of a bird's wings, then it is used of [b] the attitude of a man in prayer with his arms outstretched, and finally of [c] a human form stretched upon a cross (74).

Overwhelmingly the Church Fathers and early apocryphal material interpreted "the sign of the Son of man in the heaven" (Matt 24:30) in terms of the third meaning (Harris 75–77) and accordingly imagined that the crucified Christ or a cross carried by an angel would constitute the terrible sign of the final coming. Taylor, in his early commentary, thus rendered the obscure text as "the sign of a (cross) spreading out in heaven" (101–103). While scholars have been troubled[9] by reading patristic material back into the *Didache*, no attractive alternative has captured their attention.

---

[9] Scholars such as Harris (75), Audet (473–74), and Giet (253 n. 38) expressed hesitation in identifying the first sign with "the cross." Recent scholars such as Rordorf (1978a and 1998:198) and Niederwimmer (1989:224), however, have reviewed the known alternatives and have come to the conclusion that Taylor's original position is probably correct.

The notion that the cross was taken up into heaven with Jesus was first related in the *Gospel of Peter* (mid-second century). If the *Didache* had been composed in the mid-second century as has been supposed for so long, it would be possible to allow that the legend of the cross just noted might have been understood behind the obscure first sign of truth. Even though Rordorf and Niederwimmer both date the *Didache* as having been composed, at the latest, at the opening of the second century (Rordorf 1998:245; Niederwimmer 1998:43), neither of them appears to give much weight to the late evidence for the legend of the cross. Even in the commentaries on Matthew the identification of the "sign of the Son of Man" with the cross can be

In 1993 Jonathan Draper offered an attractive alternative reading of the first sign. Draper took his point of departure not from the Church Fathers, but from the prophetic literature of Israel. He carefully noted that the setting up of a standard or flag was "usually accompanied" (1993:7) by the sounding of a shofar or trumpet. The sounding of the shofar(s) served to signal that the people were to assemble; the flag showed where they were to assemble (Isa 5:26; 11:10-12; 13:2; 31:9; 62:10; Jer 51:27). The sounding of a shofar/trumpet is thus a common feature in eschatological settings even when the raising of a totem/flag is not mentioned (Isa 27:13; Joel 2:1; Zeph 1:14-16; Zech 9:14; Matt 24:31; Rev 1:10; 4:1; 8:2, 6, 7, 8, 10, 12, 13; 9:1, 13, 14; 10:7; 11:15; *TDNT* 7:80–88). On the basis of these observations a fresh solution opens up for the signs in the *Didache*. The first sign—the *ekpetasis* ("the spreading out") of a flag in the heavens—is intimately associated with the second sign, the sounding of a trumpet. The tenth benediction of the *Shemoneh ʿEsreh* used in the synagogue petitions the Lord to use these very same signs (in reverse order) to gather his people on the last day:

> Sound the great trumpet to announce our freedom; set up a banner to collect our captives, and gather us together from the four corners of the earth. Blessed art thou, O Lord, who gathers the dispersed of your people Israel.

This interpretation of the first two signs has the advantage of providing an unexpected solution to another puzzling problem. The eucharistic prayers of the *Didache* in two places make direct appeal to the Father that "your church be gathered together from the ends of the earth into your kingdom" (9:4; 10:5). It would be strange, accordingly, to find no reference to this ingathering in the apocalyptic vision of this same community. Thus Draper not only supplies a satisfying alternative that is consistent with the internal logic of *Didache* 16 but, in addition, offers a link with the eucharistic expectation, namely, the ingathering of the elect. In effect, therefore, after passing through the burning-process those who have been purified receive the signal to assemble.

---

dated no earlier than the opening decades of the second century (Dinkler 77–87; Hill 108–15). For me, however, the most pressing reason to abandon the notion that the *Didache* envisioned the cross coming from heaven is the recognition that the soteriology of the cross finds no place within the internal logic of the text itself.

The sounding of the Lord's trumpet calls not only those "holy ones" who are living but also the "holy ones" raised from the dead. For all concerned, therefore, the "unfurling banner in heaven" designates *the place* where the Lord God intends to come to dwell among his people (16:8). In the Jewish prophetic and apocalyptic literature Jerusalem is the center of the world, where the Lord God will assemble his people in the last days. This may help to explain why, in Jewish apocalyptic literature, the sounding of the shofar suffices. The *Didache*, for its part, silently and deliberately passes over any mention of Jerusalem[10] both in its eschatological scenario and in its eucharistic prayers. The presumption must be, accordingly, that the Lord God will signal where the elect will be assembled through the use of his unfurling banner. All in all, therefore, if Draper's observations are accepted, many unexpected things quickly fall into place.

At the very end the Lord God will appear, like a triumphant monarch, arriving on the clouds (his chariot) with the "holy ones" forming a kind of reception committee or imperial guard (Gundry 1987:163; Hanson 375; Meyers 430). In effect, however, the Lord God has already been actively present in the burning process of testing (16:5), in the gathering of the elect, and in the raising of the righteous dead (16:6) (#15d). This is a common feature within Jewish literature: "For his visitation, God uses underlying forces which form a second level, a level of efficacious powers" (Koch 64). Thus the sign of the unfurling banner and the sounding trumpet indicate that the Lord will gather his elect in the place he chooses, where the righteous dead will be raised to life (or, alternately, where they will congregate, once raised from their sleep). Everything, then, will be in readiness for the Lord's arrival on the clouds of heaven to that place.

Overall Unity of the Didache

Initially the ordering of the material in the *Didache* may seem ragged and confusing. Upon careful examination, however, one can discover

---

[10] In the Christian *Book of Revelation* the "new Jerusalem" where God "lives among men" (Rev 21:3) is not equated with the historical Jerusalem, for the "holy city" is seen "coming down from God out of heaven" (Rev 21:2). The theme of a "new Jerusalem" already established in heaven also finds its Jewish adherents (2 *Esdras* 8:52; 10:27; *Syriac Apocalypse of Baruch* 4:1-6).

the organizational thread that accounts for the flow of topics and reveals the marvelous unity hidden below the surface from beginning to end. This is the same organizational thread that those who originally recited the *Didache* relied upon for ordering their recitation. The organizational thread is this: the *Didache* unfolds the comprehensive, step-by-step program used for the formation of a gentile convert.[11] By following the order of the *Didache*, mentors training novices were assured of following the comprehensive and psychologically sound path that master trainers before them had created to codify their tested and proven method of apprenticing novices in the way of divine wisdom—the Way of Life.

Needless to say, while the *Didache* was an oral template memorized by mentors (and, with the unfolding of the training, by their candidates as well), no one ought to imagine that training consisted of merely repeating the words of the masters. On the contrary, each mentor was expected to illustrate, inquire, question, listen to, and challenge his/her candidate in such a way that not only the words but the deep meanings of the Way of Life were being suitably assimilated and applied at every step. As in the case of every wise "father" or "mother," the mentor was expected to use the oral template as a reliable guide, but to present it in such a way as to take into account the particular circumstances, strengths, weaknesses, and fears being exhibited by the candidate.

The *Didache* begins immediately by offering the gentile candidate the key orientation that characterizes the Way of Life, namely, loving God and loving one's neighbor (1:2). Everything that follows is commentary designed to reveal the substance of "these words" (1:3) and to orient a gentile for full participation in the community of the saints. At every step the order of topics follows the needs of the candidate:

---

[11] As a scholar dwells within the clues of a text for a prolonged period he or she eventually comes to define an *origination hypothesis* that endeavors to account for the peculiarities of the text and to provide an overall understanding of its origin, use, and content. The formulation of this origination hypothesis and its verification (or falsification) is much more complex than is normally supposed. In my commentary (Milavec 2003) I take the time to explore and evaluate various contending origination hypotheses. Within the limitations of this brief commentary, however, such a study would be tedious and distracting. Accordingly, I have offered my origination matrix as a working hypothesis and have proceeded immediately to examine the particulars of the text. If you have developed an independent origination hypothesis or have taken the pain to critique mine, I would appreciate having you transmit a copy of your work to me at milavec@ameritech.net.

(a) Initially the pressing concern is preparing the candidate for abusive treatment at home (1:3-5); (b) midway, the language of "my child" predominates, signaling the deepening of the "father-son" or "mother-daughter" relationship (3:1-8); (c) near the end the future tense is used to prepare the candidate for the community living that he or she has not yet known (3:9–4:14). Baptism is the rite of passage (7:1-3). Just before baptism, the rule of eating is given (6:3). As the candidate is fasting (purging his or her body of food sacrificed to idols), he or she is being prepared to live the rest of his or her life (a) eating the safe food of the community table and (b) abstaining from food twice each week (8:1). At the close of the baptism the newly baptized pray the Lord's Prayer with the community for the first time (8:2) and anticipate doing the same three times each day for the rest of their lives (8:3). All, then, join in the festive first Eucharist (9–10). Given the festive character of this event, when new members are welcomed by their "family," the confession of failings normally used before the Eucharist is deliberately suppressed, and is described later (14:1-3). Given the presence of prophets at the Eucharist, something the newly baptized encounter for the first time (10:7), the extended instruction on prophets and other visitors (11:1–13:2) is given following the first Eucharist. Following this the rules for first fruits are explained and the prophets are singled out as the ones who can best be counted on to offer up rich, spontaneous prayers of gratitude to the Lord (13:3). Finally, the newly baptized (a) are prepared to participate in the confession of failings at their second and subsequent eucharists (14:1-3), (b) are alerted to the special honor due to bishops and deacons (15:1-2), something missed in the excitement of the first Eucharist, and (c) have the rules for reproving and shunning explained in detail. Participation at multiple Eucharists undoubtedly stimulates a deep concern for the eschatological hope of the community. Thus at some teachable moment the final formal task of the mentor is to explain in detail the solemn warnings (16:1-2) and the sequence of events that will culminate in the Lord's coming to establish the Kingdom (16:8).

Upon inspection, therefore, the *Didache* exhibits a remarkable unity and purpose. It opens by offering the candidate the key orientation toward love of God and love of neighbor that characterize the Way of Life. It closes by evoking the expectation of that glorious day when the Lord God will come atop the clouds of heaven (16:8) and gather into the Kingdom those whose lives have exhibited this orientation. Thus the *Didache* traces how humble beginnings anticipate an exalted end.

Questions for Review and Study[12]

1. What is the logic for affirming that "the authorship [of the *Didache*] cannot be decided on the basis of the received titles"? *In the end, therefore, given the oral character of the *Didache*, what would you surmise was the route whereby the *Didache* originated and was used? *What might have prompted the eventual need to produce a written copy?

2. How does the contrasting of "two ways" give a fundamental orientation to the novices beginning their initiation? What is the weight of contrasting "life" and "death"? *Given the fact that the Jesus movement was known in some circles as "the Way" (Acts 9:2; 19:9, 23; 22:4; 24:14, 22), does this mean that Luke-Acts knew of the *Didache* or of Didache communities?

3. When the opening lines (1:1-2) join loving God and loving neighbor, does this signal that the perspective here comes directly from Jesus? Explain. *Does defining the Way of Life as was done give any hint as to whether the Didache communities stood within Judaism, on the borders, or outside of Judaism? *What would be the strongest indication in the text that the Didache communities stood within Judaism? . . . outside of Judaism?

---

[12] Questions follow the flow of the commentary. Those questions beginning with an " * " go beyond the explicit content of this commentary and require some stretching to provide a satisfying response. Instructors should decide to what degree their students have sufficient background and ability to productively expend their energies on these latter questions. In any case, instructors will know how to select those questions that have particular relevance for their course and to revise them (as needed) accordingly.

Students are invited to go to www.Didache.info where, in the member area, they can sign on to a bulletin board that offers resources and exchanges about the *Didache*. Those stimulated by issues raised by others will be challenged to post their own responses/discoveries on topics of personal interest. The advantages are immediate. Students take ownership of their own learning and alter their point of view as the exchange proceeds. Discussions sometimes become "hot," while others simmer in the background. Moreover, experts and novices intermingle. Strangers even become friends. One steps into a global classroom without walls.

Interested persons may look at www.Didache.info and browse. Should an instructor wish to invite his or her entire class to participate, please alert the moderator (milavec@ameritech.net) a few weeks in advance so that some simple "safety rules" can be established and "secure passwords" can be arranged.

4. Why does this commentary translate the term *didachē* as "training" rather than as "teaching"? *What importance does this choice have in view of the fact that all other English translations render this term as "teaching"?

5. How does this commentary arrive at the position that the training takes place one-to-one rather than in a group setting? How does one decide whether women were being trained? If women were being trained, how does one decide whether men served as their mentors? *In the ancient world, what significance would be given to the practice of having women trained by someone other than their husbands or fathers/mothers?

6. What does it mean that "praying and fasting [1:3] functioned to provide the necessary orientation for sustaining a comprehensive nonviolent surrender to the abusive family situation" of the would-be convert? *Why does seizure of goods [1:4D] show up here?

7. How does the surrender of goods (1:5) function at this early point in the apprenticeship? What weight is given to "the Father wishes" (1:5)? *What significance should be given to the observation that the *Didache* gives no importance to the abstract nature of God (as spiritual, all-knowing, all-powerful, etc.) but, in every instance, talking about God is intimately linked to talking about the life of the candidate (as in 1:2, 1:5, 3:10)?

8. What does one learn from the altered decalogue of 2:2 about the settled habits of gentiles that will no longer be tolerated? . . . about those prohibitions of the Mosaic decalogue that cannot, in these circumstances, be required of gentiles? *Does the mentor use the decalogue to accuse and to humble the novice as "a sinner" who needs to repent? Explain.

9. The candidate is suddenly addressed as "my child" (3:1) midway in the training. What does one learn from this about the relationship that was being cultivated from the very start? How does 2:7[3] support this? Does 4:1 follow from this? Explain. *What experiences have you ever had that prompted you to acknowledge someone outside your family acting "as a father" or "as a mother" for

you? *How is your experience like and unlike that of a candidate entering a Didache community?

10. Is the training implied in 3:2-6 building on the prior training in the decalogue (2:2)? How so (or not)? Does the training in 3:2-6 represent a preparation for 3:7-10? How so (or not)? *Can you make a convincing case, therefore, that the training manual here implies a systematic progression in the training process itself such that none of these three units could be switched around?

11. Explain the significance implied in training the candidate to acknowledge "that, apart from God, nothing happens" (3:10). *How might this orientation apply to (a) the experience of facing bitter family opposition to one's new way of life and (b) the experience of gaining a "father" or "mother" during one's apprenticeship (and, eventually, of gaining new "brothers and sisters" at the time of baptism)?

12. How does 4:6-8 have a bearing on the economic well-being of everyone within the community? Based on the text itself, what difficulties can you surmise were sometimes present when it came to implementing the giving and partnering envisioned? Explain. *How does the future practice of 4:6-8 relate to the earlier practice of 1:5?

13. The handling of "failings" shows up first in 4:3, then again in 4:14, and finally receives its longest treatment in 14:1-3. Make a case for showing that these three sections on "failings" are all in their proper place and that it would have been a mistake for some editor to try to splice all of these together in one place. *If one assumes that 15:3 is well placed (rather than out of place), what significance might be given to the fact that 15:3 follows on the heels of 15:1-2?

14. What is the weight given to 6:1? Does it appear as well placed or out of place here? *How is 6:1 related to, yet significantly different from 11:1-2?

15. Why is the rule regarding permitted foods given only at the end of the training, just prior to baptism? How is this related to the practice

and experience of fasting before baptism? *According to Mark, Jesus "declared all foods clean" (Mark 7:19). What significance should be assigned to the evident difference between Mark 7:19 and *Did.* 6:2?

16. What significance should be assigned to the graded water options named in the *Didache* (7:2-3)? Who decides? *What should be made of the fact that the *Didache* appears so flexible when it comes to water (7:2-3), yet so inflexible when it comes to food (6:3)?

17. Using clues from the text alone, what can we know regarding the when, where, and how of daily prayer? *What themes in the Lord's Prayer find emphasis in the weekly Eucharist? Draw some conclusions.

18. Using clues from the prayer texts alone, what can we know regarding the where, when, and how of the Kingdom of God? *How does this differ from the way most Christians think today?

19. Using clues from the daily and eucharistic prayers, what can be known regarding how the Didache communities understood and appreciated Jesus? *What aspects of later Christian belief appear to be entirely absent from the *Didache*? *What does this say about the date of the writing?

20. The commentary says, "The impression given is that the community had more to fear from abusive and wayward prophets than to receive from true ones." Explain this. How did the community safeguard itself from false prophets? *What was the most precious gift received from true prophets? Explain.

21. What circumstances might have led prophets to settle down within the Didache communities? Why were they unsettled to begin with? Why does the commentary conclude that "the Didache community appears to attract, absorb, and in the end to dissolve the prophetic spirit itself"? *Since the *Didache* makes provision for offering first fruits even when a prophet was not present (13:4), how does this strengthen or weaken the hypothesis that the joy of living dissolved the eschatological fire of resident prophets?

22. How does it make sense that local communities appointed "bishops"? From their qualifications, what can one surmise might be the job description of bishops? *Did these bishops wear a distinctive garb or preside at the Eucharist?

23. Does the description of the end-times (16:3-8) unfold in a logical progression? Explain. What significance does the *Didache* give to "Be watchful" (16:1) and "You do not know the hour in which our Lord is coming" (16:1)? *Is "the Lord" who is expected the "Lord Jesus" or the "Lord God"? Explain.

24. Make two columns. In the first column sketch out those arguments that try to show that the "first sign" (16:6) is either Jesus crucified or his cross. In the second column sketch out those that favor an unfurling banner. Reflect for a moment and add, if you are able, one or two additional arguments not mentioned in the commentary. *Underline the argument that is most decisive for you and defend your choice.

25. What discoveries did you make that go beyond what is presented in the commentary? How and why did you arrive at them? What difficulties and objections do you have regarding positions advocated within the commentary? *What issues trouble you, for which the commentary and your classroom have offered no satisfactory solution?

Bibliography

Achtemeier, Paul J.
1990   *"Omne verbum sonat*: The New Testament and the Oral Environment of Late Western Antiquity," *JBL* 109:3–27.

Audet, Jean Paul
1958   *La Didache: Instructions des apôtres.* Paris: J. Gabalda.

Barnard, Leslie W.
1966   "The Dead Sea Scrolls, Barnabas, the *Didache* and the Later History of the 'Two Ways,'" in idem, Studies in the Apostolic Fathers and their Background. Oxford: Blackwell, 87–107.

Bauer, Walter
1979   *A Greek-English Lexicon of the New Testament and Other Early Christian Literature: A Translation and Adaptation of the Fourth Revised and Augmented Edition of Walter Bauer's Griechisch-Deutsches Wörterbuch zu den Schriften des Neuen Testaments und der übrigen urchristlichen Literatur.* Translated by William F. Arndt and F. Wilbur Gingrich. 2nd ed. revised and augmented by F. Wilbur Gingrich and Frederick W. Danker from Walter Bauer's 5th ed. Chicago: University of Chicago Press.

Bigg, Charles
1904   "Notes on the Didache," *JTS* 5:579–89.
1905   "Notes on the Didache," *JTS* 6:411–15.
1922   *The Doctrine of the Twelve Apostles* (translation and notes). London: SPCK.

Bradshaw, Paul F.
1982   *Daily Prayer in the Early Church: The Study of the Origin and Early Development of the Divine Office.* New York: Oxford University Press.
1992   *The Search for the Origins of Christian Worship.* New York: Oxford University Press.

Brown, Colin, ed.
1978   *The New International Dictionary of New Testament Theology.* 3 vols. Grand Rapids: Zondervan.

Brown, Raymond E.

1961   "The Pater Noster as an Eschatological Prayer," *TS* 22:175–208.

1967   *Jesus: God and Man.* Milwaukee: Bruce.

1970   *Priest and Bishop: Biblical Reflections.* New York: Paulist.

1980   "*Episkopē* and *Episkopos:* The New Testament Evidence," *TS* 41:322–38.

Burtchaell, James Tunstead

1992   *From Synagogue to Church: Public Services and Offices in the Earliest Christian Communities.* Cambridge: Cambridge University Press.

Campenhausen, Hans von

1969   *Ecclesiastical Authority and Spiritual Power in the Church of the First Three Centuries.* Translation by J. A. Baker of the 1953 German original. Palo Alto: Stanford: University Press.

Corley, Kathleen E.

1993   *Private Women; Public Meals: Social Conflict in the Synoptic Tradition.* Peabody, Mass.: Hendrickson.

Crossan, John Dominic

1994   *Jesus: A Revolutionary Biography.* San Francisco: HarperSanFrancisco.

1998   *The Birth of Christianity: Discovering What Happened in the Years Immediately After the Execution of Jesus.* San Francisco: HarperSanFrancisco.

Dehandschutter, Bordewijn

1995   "The Text of the Didache: Some Comments on the Edition of Klaus Wengst," in Clayton N. Jefford, ed., *The Didache in Context: Essays on Its Text, History and Transmission.* Leiden: Brill, 37–46.

Dinkler, Erich

1964   *Das Apsismosaik von S. Apollinare in Classe.* Wissenschaftliche Abhandlungen der Arbeitsgemeinschaft für Forschung des Landes Nordrhein-Westfalen 49. Cologne/Opladen: Westdeutscher Verlag.

Draper, Jonathan A.

1991   "Torah and Troublesome Apostles in the Didache Community," *NT* 33:347–72.

1993   "The Development of 'The Sign of the Son of Man' in the Jesus Tradition," *NTS* 39:1–21.

1995   "Social Ambiguity and the Production of Text: Prophets, Teachers, Bishops, and Deacons and the Development of the Jesus Tradition in the Community of the *Didache*," in Clayton N. Jefford, ed., *The Didache in Context: Essays on Its Text, History and Transmission.* Leiden: Brill, 284–312.

1996   "The Jesus Tradition in the *Didache*," in idem, ed., *The Didache in Modern Research.* Leiden: Brill, 72–91.

1997   "Resurrection and the Cult of Martyrdom in the Didache Apocalypse," *JECS* 5:155–79.

2000   "Ritual Process and Ritual Symbol in *Didache 7–10*," *VC* 54:121–58.

Dunn, James D. G.

1977   *Unity and Diversity in the New Testament: An Inquiry into the Character of Earliest Christianity.* Philadelphia: Westminster.

Fox, Robin Lane

1987   *Pagans and Christians.* New York: Alfred A. Knopf.

Freedman, David Noel, editor-in-chief

1992   *The Anchor Bible Dictionary (ABD).* 6 vols. New York: Doubleday.

Gaier, Deborah Rose

1996   "The Didache: A Community of Equals," a paper presented in the "Women and the Historical Jesus" session of the Society of Biblical Literature's 1996 Annual Meeting. Highlights summarized in Crossan 1998:369–73.

Giet, Stanislas

1970   *L'énigme de la Didache.* Publications de la Faculté des Lettres de l'Université de Strasbourg 149. Paris: Ophrys.

Grubbs, Judith Evans

1994   "'Pagan' and 'Christian' Marriage: The State of the Question," *JECS* 2/4 (1994) 361–412.

Gundry, Robert H.

1987   "The Hellenization of Dominical Tradition and Christianization of Jewish Tradition in the Eschatology of 1–2 Thessalonians," *NTS* 33:161–78.

1993   *Mark: A Commentary on His Apology for the Cross.* Grand Rapids: Eerdmans.

1994   *Matthew: A Commentary on His Handbook for a Mixed Church under Persecution.* 2nd ed. Grand Rapids: Eerdmans.

Hanson, Paul D.

1979   *The Dawn of Apocalyptic: The Historical and Sociological Roots of Jewish Apocalyptic Eschatology.* Philadelphia: Fortress.

Harnack, Adolf von

1886   *Die Lehre der Zwölf Apostel, nebst Untersuchungen zur ältesten Geschichte der Kirchenverfassung und des Kirchenrechts.* Texte und Untersuchungen zur Geschichte der Altchristlichen Literatur 2/1-2. Leipzig: J. C. Hinrichs, 1–70.

Harris, J. Rendel
1887   *The Teaching of the Apostles: Newly Edited, with Facsimile Text and a Commentary.* London: C. J. Clay.

Heinemann, Joseph
1977   *Prayers in the Talmud: Forms and Patterns.* Studia Judaica 9. Translated from the 1966 Hebrew original by Richard S. Sarasan. Berlin: Walter de Gruyter.

Henderson, Ian H.
1992   "*Didache* and Orality in Synoptic Comparison," *JBL* 111:283–306.

Hill, Julian
1990   *Tradition and Composition in the Epistula Apostolorum.* Harvard Dissertations in Religion 24. Minneapolis: Fortress.

Hitchcock, Roswell D., and Francis Brown, eds.
1884   *Teaching of the Twelve Apostles: Edited with a Translation, Introduction and Notes.* New York: Charles Scribner's Sons.

Jay, Nancy
1992   *Throughout Your Generations Forever: Sacrifice, Religion, and Paternity.* Chicago: University of Chicago Press.

Jefford, Clayton, ed.
1995   *The Didache in Context: Essays on Its Text, History and Transmission.* Leiden: Brill.

Jeremias, Joachim
1956   *Jesus' Promise to the Nations.* Translated by S. H. Hooke from the 1956 German original. Philadelphia: Fortress.
1960   *Infant Baptism in the First Four Centuries.* London: SCM.
1963   *The Origins of Infant Baptism.* London: SCM.
1971   *New Testament Theology: The Proclamation of Jesus.* Translated by John Bowden from the 1971 German original. New York: Charles Scribner's Sons.

Kavanaugh, Aidan
1976   "Christian Initiation of Adults: The Rites," in Richard P. Humbrecht, ed., *Made, Not Born: New Pespectives on Christian Initiation and the Catechumenate.* Notre Dame: University of Notre Dame Press, 118–37.

Kelber, Werner H.
1983   *The Oral and the Written Gospel.* Philadelphia: Fortress.

Kittel, Gerhard, and Gerhard Friedrich, eds.
1968   *Theological Dictionary of the New Testament (TDNT).* 10 vols. Translated by Geoffrey W. Bromiley. Grand Rapids: Eerdmans, 1964–68.

Koch, Klaus

1983   *The Prophets of the Assyrian Period.* Philadelphia: Fortress.

Kohlenberger, John R., III, ed.

1984   *The Expanded Vine's Expository Dictionary of New Testament Words.* Minneapolis: Bethany House.

Lefkowitz, Mary R. and Maureen B. Fant, compilers

1992   *Women's Life in Greece and Rome.* 2nd ed. Baltimore: Johns Hopkins University Press.

Malina, Bruce J.

1991   "Honor and Shame in Luke-Acts: Pivotal Values of the Mediterranean World," in idem and Jerome H. Neyrey, eds., *The Social World of Luke-Acts.* Peabody, Mass.: Henderickson, 25–65.

1995   *The New Testament World: Insights from Cultural Anthropology.* Rev. ed. Louisville: Westminster John Knox.

1996   "Mediterranean Sacrifice: Dimensions of Domestic and Political Religion," *BTB* 26:26–44.

Meier, John P.

1994   *A Marginal Jew: Rethinking the Historical Jesus.* Vol. 2. New York: Doubleday.

Meyers, Carol L., et al.

1993   *Zechariah 9–14.* AB 25C. New York: Doubleday.

Milavec, Aaron

1982   *To Empower as Jesus Did: Acquiring Spiritual Power Through Apprenticeship.* Lewiston: Edwin Mellen.

1989a   "The Pastoral Genius of the Didache," in Jacob Neusner, Ernest S. Rerichs, and A. J. Levine, eds., *Religious Writings and Religious Systems. Systemic Analysis of Holy Books in Christianity, Islam, Buddhism, Greco-Roman Religions, Ancient Israel, and Judaism.* Brown Studies in Religion 1, 2. Atlanta: Scholars, 2:89–125.

1989b   "Mark's Parable of the Wicked Husbandman as Reaffirming God's Predilection for Israel," *JES* 26:289–312.

1989c   "The Heuristic Circularity of Commitment and the Experience of Discovery: A Polanyian Critique of Thomas Kuhn's *Structure of Scientific Revolutions*," *Tradition and Discovery* 16:4–19.

1990   "The Identity of 'the Son' and 'the Others': Mark's Parable of the Wicked Husbandmen Reconsidered," *BTB* 20:30–37.

1992   "The Birth of Purgatory: Evidence of the *Didache*," *Proceedings of the Eastern Great Lakes Biblical Society* 12:91–104.

1993   "If I Join Forces with Mr. Kuhn": Polanyi and Kuhn as Mutually Supportive and Corrective," *Polanyiana* (Budapest) 2/4 and 3/1:56–74. Reprinted in Richard Gelwick, ed., *From Polanyi to the 21st Century. Proceedings of a*

Centennial Conference, Kent State University, April 11–13, 1997. Biddeford, Maine: Polanyi Society, 224–59.

1994a   *Exploring Scriptural Sources: Rediscovering Discipleship.* Kansas City: Sheed & Ward.

1994b   "Distinguishing True and False Prophets: The Protective Wisdom of the Didache," *JECS* 2:117–36.

1995a   "The Social Setting of 'Turning the Other Cheek' and 'Loving One's Enemies' in Light of the *Didache*," *BTB* 25:131–43.

1995b   "Saving Efficacy of the Burning Process in Didache 16.5," in Clayton N. Jefford, ed., *The Didache in Context: Essays on Its Text, History and Transmission.* Leiden: Brill, 131–55.

1996a   *Scripture Sleuth: Rediscovering the Early Church.* Interactive software version of 1994a. Liguori, Mo.: Liguori Faithware. Distributed by Easy-Greek Software, 329 W. Greene St., Piqua, Ohio 45356 (ph. 937-778-1447).

1996b   "The Economic Safety Net in the Didache," *Proceedings of the Eastern Great Lakes Biblical Society* 16:73–84.

1996c   "How the *Didache* Attracted, Cooled Down, and Quenched Prophetic Fire," *Proceedings of the Eastern Great Lakes Biblical Society* 19:103–17.

2003a   "The Purifying Confession of Failings Required by the Didache's Eucharistic Sacrifice," *BTB* 33/2:64-76.

2003b   "Synoptic Tradition in the *Didache* Revisited," *JECS* 11/4:443–80.

2003c   *The Didache: Faith, Hope, and Life of the Earliest Christian Communities 50–70 C.E.* New York: Paulist.

Neusner, Jacob

1988a   *Judaism: The Evidence of the Mishnah.* Brown Judaic Studies 129. Atlanta: Scholars.

1988b   *The Systemic Analysis of Judaism.* Brown Judaic Studies 137. Atlanta: Scholars.

1988c   *Wrong Ways and Right Ways in the Study of Formative Judaism: Critical Method and Literature, History and the History of Religion.* Brown Judaic Studies 145. Atlanta: Scholars.

Niederwimmer, Kurt

1996   "An Examination of the Development of Itinerant Radicalism in the Environment and Tradition in the *Didache*," in Jonathan A. Draper, ed., *The Didache in Modern Research.* Leiden: Brill, 321–39. Reprint and translation of "Zur Entwicklungsgeschichte des Wanderradikalismus im Traditionsbereich der Didache," *Wiener Studien* 11 (1977) 145–67.

1998   *The Didache.* Translation by Linda M. Maloney of the 1989 German original. Hermeneia. Minneapolis: Fortress.

Novak, David

1983   *The Image of the Non-Jew in Judaism: An Historical and Constructive Study of the Noahide Laws.* Lewiston: Edwin Mellen.

1989 *Jewish-Christian Dialogue: A Jewish Justification.* Oxford: Oxford University Press.

Ong, Walter J.
1967 *The Presence of the Word: Some Prolegomena for Cultural and Religious History.* Minneapolis: University of Minnesota Press.

Peterson, Erik
1959 "Über einige Probleme der Didache-Überlieferung," in idem, *Frühkirche, Judentum und Gnosis.* Rome: Herder.

Petuchowski, Jacob J.
1972 *Understanding Jewish Prayer.* New York: Ktav.

Polanyi, Michael
1964 *Personal Knowledge.* Reprint of the 1958 original. New York: Harper Torchbooks.
1966 *Tacit Dimension.* Garden City: Doubleday.

Rordorf, Willy
1978a *La doctrine des douze apôtres.* Translation of the Greek and critical notes by André Tuilier. Paris: Cerf.
1978b "The Didache," *The Eucharist of the Early Christians.* Translation by Matthew J. O'Connell of the 1976 French original, edited by Willy Rordorf et al. New York: Pueblo, 1–23. French original reprinted in *Liturgie: foi et vie des premiers chrétiens.* Paris: Beauchesne, 1986, 187–207.
1991 "Does the Didache Contain Jesus Tradition Independently of the Synoptic Gospels?" in Henry Wansbrough, ed., *Jesus and the Oral Synoptic Tradition.* Sheffield: Sheffield Academic Press, 394–423. Reprinted in Willy Rordorf, *Lex orandi lex credendi. Gesammelte Aufsätze zum 60. Geburtstag.* Paradosis 36. Fribourg: Universitätsverlag, 1993, 330–59.
1998 *La doctrine des douze apôtres.* Second edition of the 1978 original, augmented with critical notes summarizing scholarly advances during the intervening twenty years (pp. 221–46). Paris: Cerf.

Ross, H. J.
1922 "Divination," in James Hastings, ed., *Encyclopedia of Religion and Ethics.* Edinburgh: T & T Clark, 5:759–71.

Rousselle, Aline
1988 *Porneia: On Desire and the Body in Antiquity.* Translation by Felicia Pheasant of the 1983 French original. Oxford: Basil Blackwell.

Sabatier, Paul
1885 *La Didachè ou L'enseignement des douze apôtres.* Paris: Librairie Fischbacher.

Sanders, E. P.
1977   *Paul and Palestinian Judaism.* Philadelphia: Fortress.
1985   *Jesus and Judaism.* Philadelphia: Fortress.
1990   *Jewish Law from Jesus to Mishnah.* London: SCM.
1992   *Judaism: Practice and Belief 63 B.C.E.–66 C.E.* London: SCM.

Schaff, Philip
1885   *The Oldest Church Manual Called the Teaching of the Twelve Apostles.* Edinburgh: T & T Clark; New York: Funk & Wagnalls.

Schöllgen, Georg
1991   *Didache: Zwölf-Apostel-Lehre.* Fontes Christiani 1. Freiburg: Herder, 25–94.
1996   "The *Didache* as a Church Order: An Examination of the Purpose for the Composition of the *Didache* and its Consequences for its Interpretation," in Jonathan A. Draper, ed., *The Didache in Modern Research.* Leiden: Brill, 43–71. Translation of "Die *Didache* als Kirchenordnung," *JAC* 29 (1986) 5–26.

Taylor, C.
1886   *The Teaching of the Twelve Apostles with Illustrations from the Talmud.* Cambridge: Deighton Bell.

Theissen, Gerd
1977   *Sociology of Early Palestinian Christianity.* Translation by John Bowden of the 1977 German original. Philadelphia: Fortress.
1992   "Nonviolence and Love of Our Enemies," in idem, *Social Reality and the Early Christians: Theology, Ethics, and the World of the New Testament.* Translation by Margaret Kohl. Minneapolis: Fortress, 115–56.

Van de Sandt, Huub, and David Flusser
2002   *The Didache: Its Jewish Sources and Its Place in Early Judaism and Christianity.* Minneapolis: Fortress; Assen: Royal Van Gorcum.

Vööbus, Arthur
1968   *Liturgical Traditions in the Didache.* Stockholm: Estonian Theological Society in Exile.
1969   "Regarding the Background of the Liturgical Traditions in the Didache," *VC* 23:81–87.

Wengst, Klaus
1984   *Didache (Apostellehre), Barnabasbrief, Zweiter Klemensbrief, Schrift an Diognet.* Munich: Kösel.

Electronic Aids for the Study of the Didache

1. *Hearing the Didache* — In my classes I memorize and perform the *Didache* so that participants can feel the aural flow even before they read the text. *EasyGreek Software*™ has recorded my oral presentation (20 min.) and on the reverse side has recorded a feminist adaptation by Deborah Rose-Milavec. By listening to this cassette/CD as you prepare to fall asleep at night or as you travel back and forth to class, you will open yourself up to being gripped by disturbing questions and taste the thrill of making fresh discoveries for yourself. Portions of this cassette/CD might even find a suitable use in the classroom. See www.Didache.info for practical details.

2. *Interactive Software* — Most people like to discover things for themselves and not simply be told. Accordingly, I have pioneered an electronic problem-based investigation of the *Didache* that allows each individual to take charge of his or her own learning. By weaving together the mysteries of the Didache communities for oneself, one can expect to learn more easily, more enjoyably, and more deeply.

   • *Didache Explorations* is an interactive electronic Case Study that enables the student to conduct hands-on explorations of the *Didache*. Easily accessible resources open up the cultural and religious milieu in which it was framed.

   • The Warmup sparks interest, the Sleuthing empowers one to make hunches, the Debriefing consolidates and verifies results. See www.JesusWomen.com for details.

   • A Guardian Angel (consisting of hidden subroutines) watches over the user's progress and, at unexpected moments, offers encouragement, advice, confirmation in response to the user's input.

   • The user types in hunches along the way, keeps electronic journals, and engages in a debriefing interchange with the Guardian Angel.

   • Software loads effortlessly into any version of MS Windows and offers soothing colors, relaxing animation, and self-selected mood music. See www.Didache.info for details.

Flowcharts

Overview of Key Aspects of the Didache Training

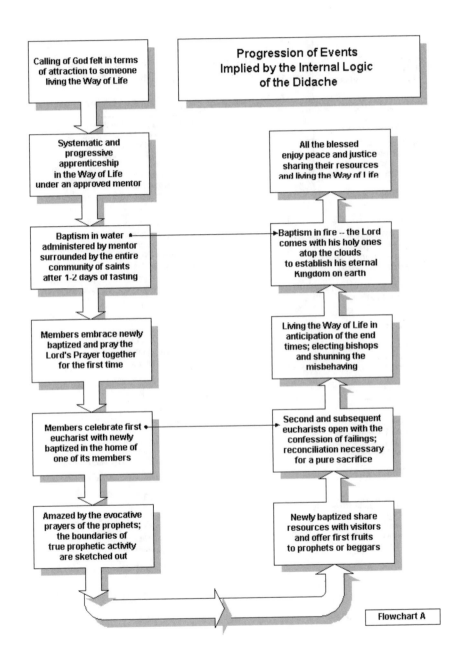

Progression of Events Implied by the Internal Logic of the Didache

Calling of God felt in terms of attraction to someone living the Way of Life

Systematic and progressive apprenticeship in the Way of Life under an approved mentor

Baptism in water administered by mentor surrounded by the entire community of saints after 1-2 days of fasting

Members embrace newly baptized and pray the Lord's Prayer together for the first time

Members celebrate first eucharist with newly baptized in the home of one of its members

Amazed by the evocative prayers of the prophets; the boundaries of true prophetic activity are sketched out

All the blessed enjoy peace and justice sharing their resources and living the Way of Life

Baptism in fire -- the Lord comes with his holy ones atop the clouds to establish his eternal Kingdom on earth

Living the Way of Life in anticipation of the end times; electing bishops and shunning the misbehaving

Second and subsequent eucharists open with the confession of failings; reconciliation necessary for a pure sacrifice

Newly baptized share resources with visitors and offer first fruits to prophets or beggars

Flowchart A

107

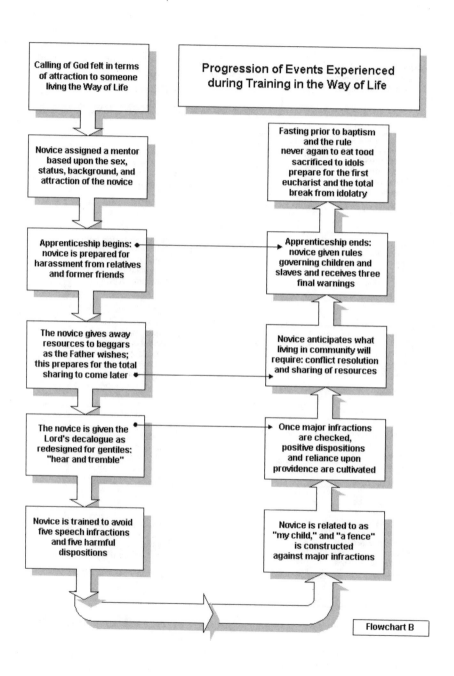

Calling of God felt in terms of attraction to someone living the Way of Life

Progression of Events Experienced during Training in the Way of Life

Novice assigned a mentor based upon the sex, status, background, and attraction of the novice

Fasting prior to baptism and the rule never again to eat food sacrificed to idols prepare for the first eucharist and the total break from idolatry

Apprenticeship begins: novice is prepared for harassment from relatives and former friends

Apprenticeship ends: novice given rules governing children and slaves and receives three final warnings

The novice gives away resources to beggars as the Father wishes; this prepares for the total sharing to come later

Novice anticipates what living in community will require: conflict resolution and sharing of resources

The novice is given the Lord's decalogue as redesigned for gentiles: "hear and tremble"

Once major infractions are checked, positive dispositions and reliance upon providence are cultivated

Novice is trained to avoid five speech infractions and five harmful dispositions

Novice is related to as "my child," and "a fence" is constructed against major infractions

Flowchart B

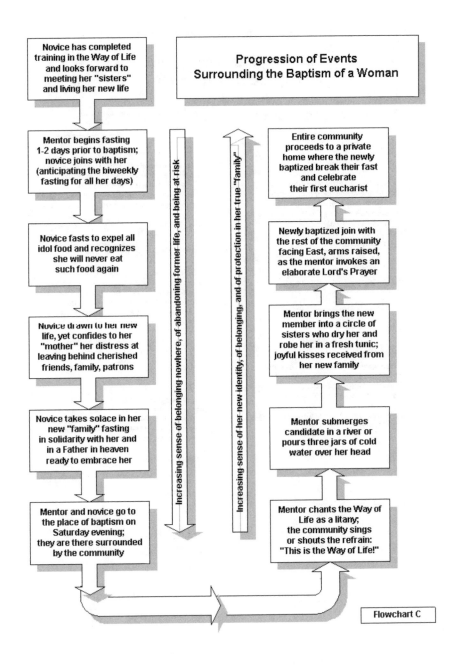

Progression of Events Surrounding the Baptism of a Woman

Novice has completed training in the Way of Life and looks forward to meeting her "sisters" and living her new life

Mentor begins fasting 1-2 days prior to baptism; novice joins with her (anticipating the biweekly fasting for all her days)

Novice fasts to expel all idol food and recognizes she will never eat such food again

Novice drawn to her new life, yet confides to her "mother" her distress at leaving behind cherished friends, family, patrons

Novice takes solace in her new "family" fasting in solidarity with her and in a Father in heaven ready to embrace her

Mentor and novice go to the place of baptism on Saturday evening; they are there surrounded by the community

Increasing sense of belonging nowhere, of abandoning former life, and being at risk

Increasing sense of her new identity, of belonging, and of protection in her true "family"

Entire community proceeds to a private home where the newly baptized break their fast and celebrate their first eucharist

Newly baptized join with the rest of the community facing East, arms raised, as the mentor invokes an elaborate Lord's Prayer

Mentor brings the new member into a circle of sisters who dry her and robe her in a fresh tunic; joyful kisses received from her new family

Mentor submerges candidate in a river or pours three jars of cold water over her head

Mentor chants the Way of Life as a litany; the community sings or shouts the refrain: "This is the Way of Life!"

Flowchart C

How Prophets Came into Being and Disappeared

How Prophets Came into Being:
(a) Expectation of the Kingdom;
(b) Experience of working harder but sinking deeper into a debt which culminated in the shameful selling of his own family into slavery;
(c) Flight to avoid capture and forced enslavement by money lenders.

How Prophets Lived:
(a) Wandering as a vagabond without provisions;
(b) Receiving short-term hospitality within Didache communities;
(c) Obsessed with the expectation of the Kingdom (fueled by their rage and longing and shame).

What Prophets Gave to their Hosts:
(a) An example of how bad things could get;
(b) A burning longing for God's future;
(c) Gratitude for the modest prosperity of their hosts as expressed in the evocative prayers offered by the prophets for first fruits.

How Some Prophets Disappeared:
(a) After becoming a permanent resident, regular eating and sleeping gradually restored their health;
(b) As their grief and rage subsided, they began to laugh and to work again;
(c) As their healing progressed, their prophetic fire naturally cooled.

What Prophets Received:
(a) Honor that lessened their shame;
(b) Lament that they had no economic safety net;
(c) When praying over the first fruits, prophets recaptured the small joys of daily living that promised to bring them healing.

Flowchart D

Progression of Events
During the End Times

Stage One:
False prophets and the
corrupters are multiplied;
"sheep turned into
wolves"

End times begin with
internal hatred and
factions fomented
by false prophets.
No menace from outside.

Stage Two:
World-deceiver does great
signs and wonders
and gains recognition
as a son of God

World-deceiver hailed!
There is no mention
of "anti-Christ," of wars,
of cosmic disturbances.

Stage Three:
All pass through the
testing fire
some destroyed;
others purified and saved

Judgment of the living!
Dual process of burning:
(a) entrapped/destroyed;
(b) purified/saved.
No role for Son of Man.

Stage Four:
"Signs of truth" =
gathering of elect &
selective resurrection

Those purified are
gathered from the four
winds and witness the
"holy ones" being raised
from the dead.

Stage Five:
The Lord-God comes;
his Kingdom brings
peace and prosperity

Together all the holy ones
triumphantly greet their
awaited Lord.
No Messiah or messianic
era anticipated.

Flowchart E

Space Provided for Your Notes